Assessing and Training Secondary School Administrators

Assessing and Training Secondary School Administrators

A Practical Workbook for Selecting Candidates
and Developing Their Skills After They're On Board

G. Steven Griggs

CORWIN PRESS, INC.
A Sage Publications Company
Thousand Oaks, California

For information:

Corwin Press, Inc.
A Sage Publications Company
2455 Teller Road
Thousand Oaks, California 91320
E-mail: order@corwinpress.com

Sage Publications Ltd.
6 Bonhill Street
London EC2A 4PU
United Kingdom

Sage Publications India Pvt. Ltd.
M-32 Market
Greater Kailash I
New Delhi 110 048 India

Printed in the United States of America

Library of Congress Cataloging-in-Publication Data

Griggs, G. Steven.
    Assessing and training secondary school administrators: A practical workbook for selecting candidates and developing their skills after they're on board /by G. Steven Griggs.
        p. cm.
    ISBN 0-8039-6893-0 (cloth: alk. paper)
    ISBN 0-8039-6894-9 (pbk.: alk. paper)
    1. School administrators—Selection and appointment—United States. 2. School administrators—Rating of—United States. 3. School administrators—In-service training—United States. 4. High schools—United States—Administration. I. Title.
    LB2831.652.G75 1999
    373.12′0071′5—dc21   99-6356

This book is printed on acid-free paper.

00 01 02 03 04 05 10 9 8 7 6 5 4 3 2 1

Editorial Assistant:	Kylee Liegl
Production Editor:	Denise Santoyo
Editorial Assistant:	Nevair Kabakian
Designer/Typesetter:	Danielle Dillahunt
Cover Designer:	Oscar Desierto

CONTENTS

3. Scenarios 49

PREFACE

▬ ▬ ▬

This book is designed to help the new or aspiring secondary administrator go beyond theory and into practice by developing solutions to problems before the problems are actually faced. Many administrators think they need to be better prepared to successfully meet the many situations that administrators encounter on a daily basis. This book is aimed at helping the new or aspiring administrator discover real-life solutions to real-life problems. It can also be used to assess the preparedness of entry-level administrative candidates.

Mail Basket Items (Chapter 2) and *Scenarios* (Chapter 3) in the book present real-life situations. Mail Basket Items are just that—items a secondary administrator could expect to receive in his or her incoming mail basket over a period of time. Scenarios are similar to Mail Basket Items but go into more depth in developing the situation at hand.

The focus of the materials in this book, as they relate to the hiring of an administrator, is how this administrator would respond to everyday situations that are faced. By asking prospective administrators to respond to these situations, the person(s) deciding who will be hired can gain insight into the candidates' decision-making skills and/or knowledge of policies, practices, guidelines, and principles. Forms are provided for candidates' responses and for evaluation of candidates' responses. Each candidate is to be given a total score on his or her responses that can then be compared with other candidates' scores.

When using the materials to train aspiring or new administrators, the *Problem-Solving Action Checklist* (Chapter 1) can be used to give the trainees "hints" for possible responses to situations. Trainees' responses can then be discussed with a mentor or teacher, and feedback can be provided. *Discussion Starter Questions* are also provided (Chapter 4) and can be used by trainers or mentors as a pathway to administrative trainees discovering the proper questions to ask on their own.

In responding to Mail Basket Items and Scenarios, the reader takes on the role of John S. Berry. Mr. Berry is the new principal of Washington

Middle/Junior High/High School. He was hired as an administrator for this school year, and he started his new position in mid-summer. Mr. Berry is 42 years old, and this is his first administrative position. He is addressed in many of the items.

A variety of reproducible forms, some of which were mentioned earlier, are provided for use in responding to the situations presented in the Mail Basket Items and Scenarios. Some forms are aimed at suggesting areas that should be considered in developing solutions to problems. Others are more open-ended and provide the user with a consistent form on which to give solutions. Still others are aimed at simply providing information that will be needed in responding to Mail Basket Items and Scenarios.

Whether you are a new or aspiring administrator, or are hiring an administrator, this book will be helpful to you. It provides a glimpse into the daily professional life of a secondary school administrator—a glimpse that can be invaluable to you in your professional future or in the future of someone who is hired.

Mail Basket and Scenario Topics

Assemblies	Library Resources
Athletic Activities	Maintenance
Attention Deficit Disorder	Medical Emergency
Budget/School Finances	Nurse/Health Issues
Bus/Transportation Issues	Parent Interactions
Communication	Professional Development
Community	Public Relations
Contributions	Scheduling
Custodial Issues	School Board Interactions
District Administration	School Relations (Neighboring School)
Drugs	School Suspension
Emergency Drills	Sex Education
Extracurricular Activities	Sexual Harassment
Field Trips	Special Education
Firearms in School	Student Discipline—General
Fund-Raising	Student-Teacher Interactions
Harassment	Support Staff Performance
In-School Suspension	Teacher Performance
Law Enforcement Involvement	Teacher Union
Legal Issues	Unauthorized Visitors

ABOUT THE AUTHOR

G. Steven Griggs (MEd, University of Missouri–St. Louis) is Associate Principal at Francis Howell Central High School in the Francis Howell School District in St. Charles, Missouri. His first experience as a certified teacher in the public schools came in 1986 at Francis Howell North High School, St. Charles, Missouri, where he taught business subjects and coached track and cross-country. He also served on the Francis Howell School District's Professional Development Committee and other building and district committees.

Griggs completed his Advanced Missouri Principal's Certification program at the University of Missouri–St. Louis in 1993 and became Assistant Principal at Barnwell Middle School that same year, where he remained for the next 3 years. In 1996, he accepted the challenge of opening a new high school in the district, Francis Howell Central, and accepted the position of Assistant Principal. He was promoted to Associate Principal of that high school in 1998.

In 1997, he discovered the need for practical professional development and assessment materials for administrators through research and communication with a variety of education professionals. He began to develop materials that were relevant and bridged the gap between the solid academic preparation that administrators receive at the university level and the daily challenges that administrators face. That initial work resulted in this book. He continues his interest in professional development by writing practical training materials for administrators and other education professionals and by conducting training seminars for educators.

EVALUATION AND ASSESSMENT FORMS

USING THE PROBLEM-SOLVING ACTION RESPONSE FORM

The *Problem-Solving Action Response Form* should be used for recording responses to Mail Basket Items, Scenarios, or both. Typically, this form is needed when these materials are being used to evaluate a candidate for an administrative position. The form can also be used if the materials are being used in a training setting and the trainer desires that trainees, without the benefit of any "hints," give responses.

If used in evaluating a candidate for an administrative position, the candidate should be given a blank *Problem-Solving Action Response Form* for each Mail Basket Item or Scenario he or she is asked to respond to, along with a copy of the actual Mail Basket Items and Scenarios. The candidate should also be given a copy of the *Partial Faculty/Staff Roster* and a copy of a filled-out *School Profile Form*.

The *Partial Faculty/Staff Roster* gives the respondent information about the faculty and staff who are referred to in some of the Mail Basket Items and Scenarios. The filled-in *School Profile Form* should reflect actual information about the school for which the new administrator is being hired and, in some instances, about the district.

The candidate should be asked to respond on a blank *Problem-Solving Action Response Form* to each situation presented to him or her. If more room is needed, the candidate can finish on the back of the form. The candidate should be told that his or her responses will be graded against a set of preestablished criteria.

Allow enough time for each candidate to respond to the Mail Basket Items and Scenarios that have been given to him or her. The amount of time needed depends on the number of situations the candidate is asked to respond to, as well as on the complexity of the Mail Basket Items and Scenarios chosen for use.

Finally, each candidate's responses should be evaluated, using a blank *Candidate Evaluation Form.*

If the *Problem-Solving Action Response Form* is to be used in a training setting, it is suggested that the *Problem-Solving Action Checklist* be used toward the beginning of the training session and the *Problem-Solving Action Response Form* toward the end of the session.

The *Problem-Solving Action Checklist* gives suggested actions that can be taken and provides a place for comments about those actions. Using this form toward the beginning of the training session will familiarize the trainee with the types of things that should be considered when formulating a response to a situation. After these skills have been developed, it is then appropriate to use the *Problem-Solving Action Response Form*, which gives no suggestions for solutions.

In this setting, even though the trainees' responses will not be evaluated as the responses of candidates for a position would be, the trainer might set up criteria on the *Candidate Evaluation Form* and have each trainee complete a self-evaluation. The *Problem-Solving Action Response Form* also gives the trainee a consistent format in which to record responses, which can be referred to later.

SAMPLE

Problem-Solving Action Response Form

NAME: _____Greg Simmons_____

MAIL BASKET / SCENARIO: __17__

DIRECTIONS: Use this form to indicate how you would respond to the *Mail Basket Item* or *Scenario* that has been given to you.

After listening to the student's complaint, and discussing it with her and the counselor, I would ask the student to write out her complaint. I would also ask her to sign and date the complaint.

I would then call the girl's parents to let them know what their daughter had reported, and to tell them how I intended to proceed from here. I would tell them that I planned to question the boy, give him a chance to respond, and discipline him according to the school's discipline code.

The girl would be sent back to class, and the boy brought in and questioned. He would be given a chance to respond to the allegations. Assuming that there was some verifiable improper action, the student would be disciplined. In any case, his parents would be contacted to let them know what had been reported and how the situation had been handled.

It would then be important to contact the girl's parents to let them know that the situation had been addressed, and to ask them to let you know if they learned of any continuing problems.

All of the above should be well documented and placed in a secure file in case it is needed for future reference.

Griggs, *Assessing and Training Secondary School Administrators.* © 2000, Corwin Press, Inc.

Problem-Solving Action Response Form

NAME: _____

MAIL BASKET / SCENARIO: _____

DIRECTIONS: Use this form to indicate how you would respond to the *Mail Basket Item* or *Scenario* that has been given to you.

_____
_____
_____
_____
_____
_____
_____
_____
_____
_____
_____
_____
_____
_____
_____
_____
_____

Griggs, *Assessing and Training Secondary School Administrators.* © 2000, Corwin Press, Inc.

USING THE PROBLEM-SOLVING ACTION CHECKLIST

The *Problem-Solving Action Checklist* should be used to record responses to Mail Basket Items and Scenarios. Typically, this form will be used in a training setting where the trainer desires that trainees develop answers with the benefit of "hints" to possible solutions.

Each trainee should be given a blank copy of the *Problem-Solving Action Checklist* for each Mail Basket Item and Scenario being discussed. A copy of each Mail Basket Item and Scenario being used in the training should also be provided to each trainee. A copy of the *Partial Faculty/Staff Roster*, along with a copy of a filled-out *School Profile Form*, should also be provided. When filling out the *School Profile Form*, the trainer should make assumptions about the school and district he or she wants the trainees to use in developing solutions. The *Partial Faculty/Staff Roster* simply provides additional information about some staff in the school referred to in the Mail Basket Items and Scenarios.

It is suggested that the trainer begin by reviewing some Mail Basket Items and Scenarios with trainees and developing solutions together in a large group setting. The large group can then be divided into smaller groups to develop solutions to other Mail Basket Items and Scenarios. Finally, trainees should have time to develop solutions to Mail Basket Items and Scenarios on their own. The larger group can then reconvene to discuss solutions.

The trainer can have trainees develop solutions on their own by using the *Problem-Solving Action Response Form*, which suggests no possible solutions but leaves the solutions up to the individual's own resourcefulness. The group can then be allowed time to reflect on each trainee's responses, thereby learning from each other.

SAMPLE
Problem-Solving Action Checklist

NAME: __Greg Simmons__   MAIL BASKET (SCENARIO): __17__

DIRECTIONS: Use this form with each *Mail Basket Item* or *Scenario* that you are responding to.
Check each of the actions below that you would take in the given situation, and note reasons behind your responses.

NOTES

☒ Conference with student   would need to talk to the girl, then to the alleged perpetrator, to verify improper actions on the boy's part

☐ Conference with employee

☐ Conference with parent (in school)

☒ Consult your immediate supervisor   let him/her know of the situation and how it was handled, since this can be a sensitive area

☐ Contact emergency personnel

☐ Contact law enforcement

☐ Contact legal counsel

☒ Contact parent   would need to contact the girl's parents & the boy's parents, then follow up to let the girl's parents know how things were handled

☐ Contact superintendent

☐ Provide family with referral list of outside agencies

(Continued)

SAMPLE
Problem-Solving Action Checklist (Continued)

[X] **Refer to school counselor** — would confer with the counselor on documenting the situation

[ ] **Refer for Special Services**

[ ] **Refer for district alternative programs (if available)**

[X] **Review building/district policies** — provide boy with copy of sexual harassment policy, and document that he had been given it

[X] **Speak with other students** — only if needed to verify information given by the boy or girl

[X] **Take disciplinary action** — boy should be disciplined according to the school's discipline code

[X] **Other (explain):** — have student write out her complaint, as documentation

[ ] **Other (explain):**

[ ] **Other (explain):**

Overall Notes on Situation:

Care should be taken to ensure that the girl's complaint is heard, that it is investigated, and that proper disciplinary and corrective action is taken. Documentation of action taken is of utmost importance, as is contact with both students' parents.

Griggs, Assessing and Training Secondary School Administrators. © 2000, Corwin Press, Inc.

Problem-Solving Action Checklist

NAME: _____

MAIL BASKET / SCENARIO: _____

DIRECTIONS: Use this form with each *Mail Basket Item* or *Scenario* that you are responding to. Check each of the actions below that you would take in the given situation, and note reasons behind your responses.

<u>*NOTES*</u>

☐ Conference with student

☐ Conference with employee

☐ Conference with parent (in school)

☐ Consult your immediate supervisor

☐ Contact emergency personnel

☐ Contact law enforcement

☐ Contact legal counsel

☐ Contact parent

☐ Contact superintendent

☐ Provide family with referral
list of outside agencies

(Continued)

Problem-Solving Action Checklist *(Continued)*

☐ Refer to school counselor

☐ Refer for Special Services

☐ Refer for district alternative
programs (if available)

☐ Review building/district policies

☐ Speak with other students

☐ Take disciplinary action

☐ Other (explain):

☐ Other (explain):

☐ Other (explain):

Overall Notes on Situation:

USING THE CANDIDATE EVALUATION FORM

The *Candidate Evaluation Form* is to be used to evaluate responses given by candidates applying for an administrative position who have been presented with Mail Basket Items and Scenarios. Candidates will have responded on the *Problem-Solving Action Response Form*.

A separate, blank *Candidate Evaluation Form* should be used for each Mail Basket Item or Scenario that the candidate is expected to respond to. The evaluator(s) who are recommending which candidate should be hired should then fill out the "Expected Response" sections in advance of candidates being presented with the situations so that the "correct" answers are preestablished. The *Sample Candidate Evaluation Form* shows how this should be done.

Expected Responses are just that—responses the evaluator(s) would expect the successful candidate to be able to develop. For example, if the Mail Basket Item or Scenario involves a disciplinary issue, one Expected Response is to contact the student's parent or guardian. Each *Candidate Evaluation Form* has room for eight Expected Responses. If more Expected Responses are required by the evaluator(s), a second *Candidate Evaluation Form* can be used.

After each candidate has been given a chance to respond, each response to each Mail Basket Item or Scenario is "graded" by the evaluator(s). The candidate is given a score of *Poor* (1) to *Excellent* (5) on each Expected Response. The candidate can also be given a score of zero on an Expected Response if no number is circled for that response. The Expected Responses are then tallied, and the candidate is given a total score for all Expected Responses. Notes may also be written on the overall quality of the candidate's answers.

If a group of evaluators is responsible for evaluating each candidate, each evaluator can fill out a *Candidate Evaluation Form* for each Mail Basket Item or Scenario used, or the group can come to consensus and use one form for the group. If each evaluator fills out a separate form, the total score on the forms can be averaged and this score recorded on the *Candidate Evaluation Recap Form*. Otherwise, the total score from the group's form can be placed on the *Candidate Evaluation Recap Form*.

SAMPLE
Candidate Evaluation Form

NAME: _Greg Simmons_   MAIL BASKET / (SCENARIO): _17_

DIRECTIONS: Use this form with each *Mail Basket Item* or *Scenario* that you are asking a candidate to respond to. Make sure that expected acceptable responses to each item are determined before the evaluation process begins.

Circle below for each expected response.

	Poor	Below Average	Average	Above Average	Excellent

Expected Response:
Parent of the girl should be contacted early in the process.

1	2	3	4	(5)

Expected Response:
Situation should be investigated after hearing complaint, including questioning witnesses.

1	2	(3)	4	5

No witnesses questioned

Expected Response:
Parent of boy should be contacted.

1	2	3	4	(5)

Expected Response:
Boy should be disciplined according to the district's discipline policy.

1	2	(3)	4	5

specific discipline not mentioned

(continued)

SAMPLE

CANDIDATE EVALUATION FORM *(continued)*

	Poor	Below Average	Average	Above Average	Excellent
Expected Response: Every step taken should be documented	1	2	3	4	⑤

Mentioned twice, and had student write complaint.

	Poor	Below Average	Average	Above Average	Excellent
Expected Response: Superintendent should be informed of the situation.	1	2	3	4	5

Did not say anything about contacting superintendent.

	Poor	Below Average	Average	Above Average	Excellent
Expected Response:	1	2	3	4	5

	Poor	Below Average	Average	Above Average	Excellent
Expected Response:	1	2	3	4	5

Poor	Below Average	Average	Above Average	Excellent
0	0	6	0	15

TOTAL SCORE OF ALL EXPECTED RESPONSES: | 21 | =

NOTES ON CANDIDATE'S OVERALL QUALITY OF ANSWERS:

Candidate did an overall good job on the situation. He shows some lack of knowledge of the school's policies, which is indicative of a lack of experience.

Griggs, *Assessing and Training Secondary School Administrators.* © 2000, Corwin Press, Inc.

Candidate Evaluation Form

NAME: _____

MAIL BASKET / SCENARIO: _____

DIRECTIONS: Use this form with each *Mail Basket Item* or *Scenario* that you are asking a candidate to respond to. Make sure that expected acceptable responses to each item are determined before the evaluation process begins.

Circle below for each expected response.

	Poor	Below Average	Average	Above Average	Excellent
Expected Response: _____ _____	1	2	3	4	5
Expected Response: _____ _____	1	2	3	4	5
Expected Response: _____ _____	1	2	3	4	5
Expected Response: _____ _____ _____	1	2	3	4	5

(continued)

Griggs, *Assessing and Training Secondary School Administrators.* © 2000, Corwin Press, Inc.

Candidate Evaluation Form (continued)

	Poor	Below Average	Average	Above Average	Excellent
	1	2	3	4	5

Expected Response: _____

_____

	Poor	Below Average	Average	Above Average	Excellent
	1	2	3	4	5

Expected Response: _____

_____

	Poor	Below Average	Average	Above Average	Excellent
	1	2	3	4	5

Expected Response: _____

_____

	Poor	Below Average	Average	Above Average	Excellent
	1	2	3	4	5

Expected Response: _____

_____

TOTAL SCORE OF ALL EXPECTED RESPONSES: [ ] = [ ]

Poor	Below Average	Average	Above Average	Excellent

NOTES ON CANDIDATE'S OVERALL QUALITY OF ANSWERS:

Griggs, *Assessing and Training Secondary School Administrators.* © 2000, Corwin Press, Inc.

USING THE CANDIDATE EVALUATION RECAP FORM

Use the *Candidate Evaluation Recap Form* for tallying the total scores from each Mail Basket Item or Scenario used in the evaluation process. Simply use one line to record the total score from each *Candidate Evaluation Form.* Total these numbers to calculate a "Candidate Grand Total" (refer to the *Sample Candidate Evaluation Recap Form*).

The Candidate Grand Total section gives the evaluator(s) one measure of each candidate's strengths and provides one means of comparing candidates. This process should be used as only one means of evaluating the overall strength of each candidate. Other areas of assessment of candidates' worthiness for the job include oral communication, past experience, other written communication, organizational skills, and professional preparation.

The "General Notes Regarding Candidate's Responses" section can be used for recording any observations that have been made about the candidate's responses that would be useful in the overall evaluation of the candidate.

SAMPLE

Candidate Evaluation Recap Form

CANDIDATE NAME: Greg Simmons

DIRECTIONS: Use this form to tally each candidate's scores from the *Candidate Evaluation Form*.

General Notes
Regarding Candidate's Responses

Communicates well.

Does not use all resources available.

Lack of knowledge of policies/procedures.

Involves parents in decisions.

Fair, firm, and consistent regarding
discipline.

TOTALS FROM Scenario #17	21
TOTALS FROM Scenario #21	13
TOTALS FROM Scenario #27	15
TOTALS FROM Mail Basket #7	25
TOTALS FROM Mail Basket #4	10
TOTALS FROM Mail Basket #15	10
TOTALS FROM	
TOTALS FROM	
TOTALS FROM	
CANDIDATE GRAND TOTAL	94

Griggs, *Assessing and Training Secondary School Administrators*. © 2000, Corwin Press, Inc.

Candidate Evaluation Recap Form

CANDIDATE NAME: _____

DIRECTIONS: Use this form to tally each candidate's scores from the *Candidate Evaluation Form* .

**General Notes
Regarding Candidate's Responses**

TOTALS FROM _____ ☐

TOTALS FROM _____ ☐

TOTALS FROM _____ ☐

TOTALS FROM _____ ☐

TOTALS FROM _____ ☐

TOTALS FROM _____ ☐

TOTALS FROM _____ ☐

TOTALS FROM _____ ☐

TOTALS FROM _____ ☐

CANDIDATE GRAND TOTAL ☐

USING THE SCHOOL PROFILE FORM

Whether the Mail Basket Items and Scenarios are being used for training purposes or for assessment purposes, people responding to the situations will at times need more information about the school and district in which these situations take place. The *School Profile Form* provides some of this information.

In preparation for using the Mail Basket Items and Scenarios, a *School Profile Form* should be completed. It is simply a check-off form that gives the respondent information about the school and the district. For each category, the proper attributes should be checked off and a copy of this completed form given to each candidate or trainee. A *Sample School Profile Form* is provided.

SAMPLE
School Profile Form

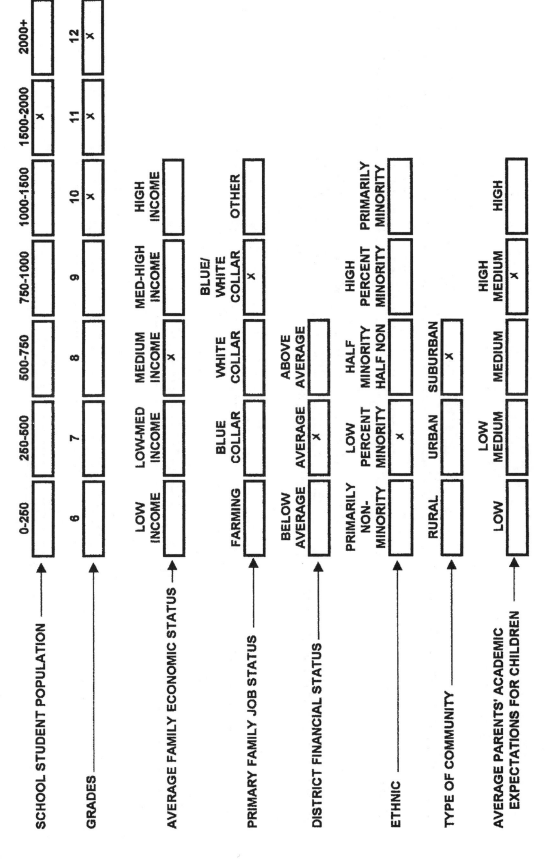

SCHOOL STUDENT POPULATION →

0-250	250-500	500-750	750-1000	1000-1500	1500-2000	2000+
					x	

GRADES →

6	7	8	9	10	11	12
				x	x	x

AVERAGE FAMILY ECONOMIC STATUS →

LOW INCOME	LOW-MED INCOME	MEDIUM INCOME	MED-HIGH INCOME	HIGH INCOME
		x		

PRIMARY FAMILY JOB STATUS →

FARMING	BLUE COLLAR	WHITE COLLAR	BLUE/ WHITE COLLAR	OTHER
			x	

DISTRICT FINANCIAL STATUS →

BELOW AVERAGE	AVERAGE	ABOVE AVERAGE
	x	

ETHNIC →

PRIMARILY NON- MINORITY	LOW PERCENT MINORITY	HALF MINORITY HALF NON	HIGH PERCENT MINORITY	PRIMARILY MINORITY
	x			

TYPE OF COMMUNITY →

RURAL	URBAN	SUBURBAN
		x

AVERAGE PARENTS' ACADEMIC EXPECTATIONS FOR CHILDREN →

LOW	LOW MEDIUM	MEDIUM	HIGH MEDIUM	HIGH
			x	

Griggs, *Assessing and Training Secondary School Administrators.* © 2000, Corwin Press, Inc.

School Profile Form

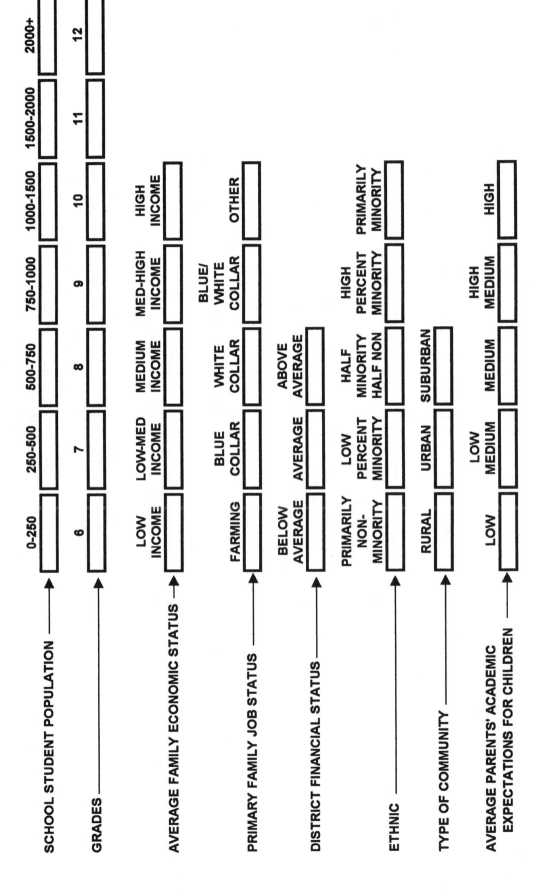

SCHOOL STUDENT POPULATION	0-250	250-500	500-750	750-1000	1000-1500	1500-2000	2000+
GRADES	6	7	8	9	10	11	12

AVERAGE FAMILY ECONOMIC STATUS	LOW INCOME	LOW-MED INCOME	MEDIUM INCOME	MED-HIGH INCOME	HIGH INCOME

PRIMARY FAMILY JOB STATUS	FARMING	BLUE COLLAR	WHITE COLLAR	BLUE/ WHITE COLLAR	OTHER

DISTRICT FINANCIAL STATUS	BELOW AVERAGE	AVERAGE	ABOVE AVERAGE

ETHNIC	PRIMARILY NON-MINORITY	LOW PERCENT MINORITY	HALF MINORITY HALF NON	HIGH PERCENT MINORITY	PRIMARILY MINORITY

TYPE OF COMMUNITY	RURAL	URBAN	SUBURBAN

AVERAGE PARENTS' ACADEMIC EXPECTATIONS FOR CHILDREN	LOW	LOW MEDIUM	MEDIUM	HIGH MEDIUM	HIGH

20

Griggs, *Assessing and Training Secondary School Administrators.* © 2000, Corwin Press, Inc.

USING THE PARTIAL FACULTY/STAFF ROSTER

Whether the Mail Basket Items and Scenarios are being used for training purposes or for assessment purposes, those responding to the situations will at times need more information about the faculty/staff referred to. The *Partial Faculty/Staff Roster* provides some of this information. A copy of this form should be given to each candidate or trainee before he or she is expected to respond to Mail Basket Items or Scenarios. The form is only a partial listing, and some faculty or staff referred to may not be listed.

Partial Faculty/Staff Roster

Name	Position	Time in Current Position	Facts About Individual
Alberta, Linda	Physical Education Teacher	8 yrs.	Softball coach
Berry, John S.	Principal	1st Year	42-year-old first-time administrator
Druid, Sheila	Language Arts Teacher	5 yrs.	Student Council sponsor
Greer, Terry	Academic Counselor	7 yrs.	Former art teacher
Grover, Gina	School Nurse	6 yrs.	Hospital nurse 6 yrs. prior to school nurse job
Honet, Karen	Science Teacher	9 yrs.	Science Department chairperson
Jenkins, Ron	Physical Education Teacher	15 yrs.	Basketball and soccer coach
Lee, Susan	Special Education Teacher	10 yrs.	Special Education Department chairperson
Masterson, Wanda	Math Teacher	1 yr.	Graduated from college last year
Matson, John	Social Studies Teacher	6 yrs.	Boys' track coach
McLafferty, Jan	Band Teacher	22 yrs.	Retires next year
Portle, Michael	Math Teacher	19 yrs.	Teachers' Social Committee chairperson
Potter, Danielle	Math Teacher	3 yrs.	Math Club sponsor
Robles, James	Science Teacher	17 yrs.	No extra duties
Smith, Joan	Language Arts Teacher	8 yrs.	Sponsors many school clubs
Stevens, Jon	Science Teacher	2 yrs.	Teacher of the Year candidate
Stiles, Tom	Teacher Aide	2 yrs.	Baseball coach
Suarez, Maria	Math Teacher	12 yrs.	No extra duties
Taley, Stephanie	Special Education Teacher	3 yrs.	No extra duties
Taylor, Betty	Principal's Secretary	15 yrs.	School secretary for 28 yrs.
Throm, Susan	Math Teacher	16 yrs.	Professional Development Committee chairperson
Wade, James	Custodian	18 yrs.	Head of local custodians' union
Weems, Charlene	Science Teacher	12 yrs.	No extra duties

Griggs, *Assessing and Training Secondary School Administrators.* © 2000, Corwin Press, Inc.

MAIL BASKET ITEMS

2

USING THE MAIL BASKET ITEMS

The items presented in this chapter are typical of the types of situations that middle school, junior high school, and high school administrators deal with on a daily basis. These items represent what a principal might expect to receive in her or his mail basket over a period of time.

In using these Mail Basket Items, for whatever reason, the respondent takes on the role of John S. Berry. Mr. Berry is the new principal of Washington Middle/Junior High/High School. He was hired as an administrator for this school year, and he started his position in mid-summer. Mr. Berry is referred to in many of the Mail Basket Items.

These items are not intended to be of an in-depth case study nature. Rather, taken as a group, they are meant to represent the diversity of situations a secondary school administrator must face on a daily basis. Some Mail Basket Items are simple and require rather simple solutions. Others take more thought and may even lead the reader to ask questions about the situation that cannot be answered from the information in the Mail Basket Item.

All Mail Basket Items should cause the reader to reflect on how she or he would respond to the situations. A major component of each response is formulating the questions for which answers must be found before a response can be given. Through a process of reflection, application of prior academic training, and experience, the reader will be able to ask the appropriate questions and give the "correct" responses to these hypothetical situations. Through this process, the reader will be better equipped to handle what she or he will face in the real world of secondary school administration.

To help users begin to ask the proper questions on their own, Discussion Starter Questions can be found in Chapter 4. These questions may be used in a variety of ways but are especially helpful in the beginning stages of aspiring administrator training programs.

186 S. Water Street
Right City, MO 63333

October 7, xxxx

Mr. John S. Berry, Principal
123 School Street
Right City, MO 63333

Dear Mr. Berry:

I wanted to follow up the conversation that I had with you the other day when I visited your school with this letter.

If you recall our conversation, I spoke with you about students from your school cutting across my property when they leave school in the afternoon to go home. The corner of my property touches the edge of the school's property near the athletic fields.

The students cause no problems when they are on my property, except that they are wearing a path in my lawn, which causes an eyesore in the spring when that area becomes a mudhole. I don't want to call the police, and hope that my talking to you and writing this letter will help you to remember to say something to these students and to discipline them if you have to in order to rectify the situation.

I thank you in advance for your help in this matter.

Sincerely,

Robert Kyle

Robert Kyle

Dear Principle

Yesterday my boy John got threatened at skool by a bigger boy. My boy comes to skool to learn, not too be picked on. He didn't due nothin back.

I want that other boy suspended from skool, like was done to John when he got a fight. If you don't due nothing too him today, I'll be up at your skool first thing in the morning. I'll call the Supertendant, to.

Call me at home at 976-2345 to let me know what you done about this.

Mr. Smith

For:	Mr. Berry		
Date:	10/9/xx	Time:	8:15 AM

WHILE YOU WERE OUT

Detective Jim Noble

Of:	County Sheriff Dept.
Phone:	745-1896

Please return call regarding:

Wants to come to school to question one of our students, Judy James, about an incident that happened outside of school.

Signed: *st*

KAREN HONET
SCIENCE DEPARTMENT CHAIRPERSON

Memo

TO: Mr. Berry

FROM: Karen Honet
             Science Department Chairperson

DATE: October 10, xxxx

RE: Budget Deadline

I wanted to let you know that I did not meet today's budget deadline (refer to your memo dated August 15, 19xx) because of some things that are beyond my control.

I called some vendors last week to ask for catalogs so that I could get prices on some of the items that I need to include in the budget for my department, but I have yet to receive the catalogs. I will give you the information as soon as I hear from the companies that I have contacted.

Please let me know if you have any questions.

From the Desk of *Mrs. McLafferty*

Mr. Berry,

I would like to take my Band students to the elementary school to do a program for them.

This would give our music department a boost, and would entertain their youngsters.

I would need to have a substitute for the day, and about 40 of my students would be out of school all day.

I'll wait to hear from you.

P.S. – just so you know, we've done this every year for the past 10 years.

Jan

PROGRAMS FOR STUDENTS   Joshua 24:15

P.O. BOX 133
GOODLAND, IL 64018
1-800-PROGRAM

October 13, xxxx

Mr. John Berry, Principal
Washington High School
123 Right Street
Right City, MO 63333

Dear Mr. Berry:

In speaking with the head of your Language Arts department, Mrs. Sheila Druid, she indicated that you would be interested in our organization coming to your school to conduct a whole-school assembly on drug abuse. As I explained to her, the program will be presented from a Christian perspective, and will include scriptural references found in the Holy Bible to support the theme that DRUG ABUSE WILL DESTROY YOU.

The cost of the 45-minute program will be $600, and will include handouts for each of your students that contain all of the scriptural references from the Bible used in the presentation, along with other facts that will help your students to avoid the pitfalls of drug abuse.

I have set aside two possible dates for our program at your school, and am anxious to speak with you about which date will work best for you. Mrs. Druid was so excited about the prospect of having our organization do a presentation at you school that she has already forwarded a $100 deposit to us, which she paid out of her own pocket!

Please call me at our 1-800 number listed above as soon as you receive this letter!

Sincerely,

John Hanes

Johnny L. Hanes
President

Memorandum

TO: John Berry, Principal

FROM: Susan Throm, Chairperson
           Professional Development Committee

DATE: October 15, xxxx

RE: November's Professional Development Activity

The Professional Development Committee is considering what should be done for next month's Professional Development activity, which is scheduled for after school on November 18.

The six members of the Committee think that a worthwhile activity would be to do a needs assessment to determine what the faculty's interests are in terms of professional development activities for the remainder of the year. This activity should not take much time after school on the 18th, and we believe that it would be a great benefit to have this information.

We also think that it is very important for every staff member to be at the meeting, including those who coach after school. Do you have any ideas on how to include them? We've tried morning meetings, and that just does not work, as many teachers have a hard time getting here early because of childcare, etc.

We would like to have your input on this idea. Please send me a note with your thoughts, or stop by to see me at your convenience.

From the desk of . . .

Jon Stevens

10/16/xx

Mr. Berry -

I have had a problem with the heat in my room for the past two weeks—since our recent cold snap. I have filled out two separate work orders about this problem, but no one has looked into it, as far as I know. It's becoming difficult for the students to learn in this environment, and I think I'm beginning to get sick from it.

Help!

Jon

WASHINGTON SCHOOL DISTRICT
DISCIPLINE NOTICE

STUDENT NAME	DATE	TEACHER
Jenny Taylor	*10~18~xx*	*Masterson*

OFFENSE

		EXPLAIN OFFENSE
CLASSROOM DISRUPTION		*Jenny was looking at a "cheat sheet"*
CHEATING	*x*	*while taking her math test. She will receive*
TARDIES TO CLASS		*a zero.*
TRUANT FROM CLASS		
TRUANT FROM SCHOOL		
OTHER		

PRINCIPAL COMMENTS

_____

_____

_____

_____

SIGNATURES

Jenny Taylor	*W. Masterson*	
Student	Teacher	Principal

For:	Mr. Berry		
Date:	10/18/xx	Time:	9:17 AM

WHILE YOU WERE OUT

Mr. Skipavovich

Of:

Phone: 746-7887

Please return call regarding:
Son John was suspended today for truancy on Monday. Wants to contest this, since John has already missed too much school.

Wants to discuss alternatives

Signed: st

Mr. Berry,

I wanted to write you a note to let you know that I believe that the janitors have been smoking in the school's boiler room. This is happening during their breaks in the evening. I knew that since the school board has put an emphasis on all of our campuses being smoke-free, you would want to know about this.

Please see me if you need more information.

John Matson

P.S. – Please don't let them know that I told you.

Education is the door
to a successful future. . .
OPEN IT!

From the Desk of
Mrs. Greer, Counselor

John,

I got a call from Mrs. Wilson today regarding Bradley's Attention Deficit Disorder. She feels that his ADD in negatively affecting his schoolwork, which may be the case from looking at his grades.

Mrs. Wilson claims that one of Bradley's biggest problems is his inability to keep up with taking notes, which is required in several of his classes. Therefore, Mrs. Wilson is requesting that Bradley be permitted to bring a tape recorder to each class to use to record teachers' lectures.

I have not spoken with any of the teachers about this yet.

Mrs. Wilson's telephone number is 989-4567. Let's get together on this before you call her.

Thanks,

Terry Greer

Terry Greer
10/20/xx

For:	Mr. Berry		
Date:	10/21/XX	Time:	2 pm

WHILE YOU WERE OUT

Steve Johnson

Of:	Johnson & Assoc. Law Firm
Phone:	789-2498

Please return call regarding:
Would like to donate $10,000
to school. Wants to talk about how
the school can help him by providing
a mailing list.

Signed:	c/m

WASHINGTON SCHOOL DISTRICT
DISCIPLINE NOTICE

STUDENT NAME	DATE	TEACHER
JOAN DIAZ	10/26/xx	L. ALBERTA

OFFENSE

		EXPLAIN OFFENSE
CLASSROOM DISRUPTION		FIGHTING. JOAN SAID THAT JEAN
CHEATING		PHILIPS CALLED HER A B_____
TARDIES TO CLASS		AND SHE RESPONDED BY HITTING HER
TRUANT FROM CLASS		IN THE FACE. I THINK JEAN'S NOSE
TRUANT FROM SCHOOL		MAY BE BROKEN.
OTHER	×	

PRINCIPAL COMMENTS

_____

_____

_____

_____

SIGNATURES

Joan Diaz	L. Alberta	
Student	Teacher	Principal

For:	Mr. Berry		
Date:	11/1/xx	Time:	12:30 PM

WHILE YOU WERE OUT

Dr. Wayne

Of:	Superintendent.
Phone:	745-1985

Please return call regarding:
Needs information about girl
who was suspended last week. Parent
called him.

Student is Jill Farn.

Signed: st

WASHINGTON SCHOOL DISTRICT
DISCIPLINE NOTICE

STUDENT NAME	DATE	TEACHER
Steven Sorta	11/18/xx	Portle

OFFENSE		EXPLAIN OFFENSE
CLASSROOM DISRUPTION	X	Student continues to ask _dumb_ questions just to interrupt class. Parents have been contacted about this in the past.
CHEATING		
TARDIES TO CLASS		
TRUANT FROM CLASS		
TRUANT FROM SCHOOL		
OTHER		

PRINCIPAL COMMENTS

SIGNATURES

Steve Sorta	Portle	
Student	Teacher	Principal

10/20/xx

Mrs. Honet,

My son, Dave Simmons, has had an unusually high level of homework from you this year. Dave is bright, but even with a tutor (his older brother who is in college), he's working on your homework from right after school until 9 in the evening. This is ridiculous.

Yesterday was the straw that broke the camel's back. After having the flu and 102 fever, Dave was able to return to school. YOU sent home three chapters of science work. This is over 10 hours of homework, not to mention the lab that he will also have to make up.

Your lack of judgment is both appalling and infuriating. My son has other classes to study for, and he has responsibilities at home.

Your job is to educate, NOT to fill up every waking minute of a kid's life with homework.

You will be hearing from me today!

Donna Smith

Ms. Donna Smith

Mr. Berry,
I received this today from one of my students, David Simmons.
This part makes me mad!
What should I do?

Karen Honet

Mr. Berry,

I am unhappy about the amount of time that students are out of my classes due to field trips. This past week alone, I had six students miss class. Three of these absences were during labs, and I had to stay after so that these students could make up the labs. One of the students stated that he could not stay after school to make up labs, because he had other commitments immediately after school.

I would like to talk to you about this.

Jim Robles

John,

I have a friend whose son is looking for a position as a science teacher. I know that you have an opening in that area due to Mr. Johnson's recent illness and resignation.

I am writing to ensure that this young man, Mark Lusecky, gets an interview with you, and would appreciate it if you would give special consideration to him when you make your hiring selection.

I was instrumental in your hiring as principal, and am just asking you to help me as you have a chance to return the favor.

Thank you so much!

Jan Kominski

School Board Member

For:	Mr. Berry		
Date:	11/22/XX	Time:	7:45 am

WHILE YOU WERE OUT

Mrs. Stephenson

Of:	Jason Stephonson's mother
Phone:	789-2513

Please return call regarding:
Wants to see you at 8:30—wants a call back right away. Is upset about a comment that a teacher made to her son.

Signed: c/m

11/21/XX

Mr. Berry—

On a regular basis, I send assignments to the In School Suspension teacher, and I routinely DO NOT receive those assignments back if or when they are completed by the student.

I REFUSE to send any more assignments to the In School Suspension teacher until this situation is resolved.

I will wait to hear from you.

Joan Smith

John,

I tried to catch you this morning, but you were in a meeting. I wanted to let you know right away about a call that I received last evening.

You may or may not know this, but we showed a video of a live human birth in all of our health classes this week, as part of our human sexuality unit. This is an excellent video that shows a woman, in a hospital setting, going through labor and giving birth. It shows all of the monitors and everything that is done in labor and delivery. The video ends with the actual birth of a beautiful baby boy.

The video is done very tastefully, but does show the entire actual birth (which lasts several minutes). I will say that it leaves nothing to the imagination.

To get to the point, the phone call was from a parent who is very upset that we showed this video to her sixteen year old boy. I indicated to her that she had to sign off on his class registration form, which indicated that she knew that he was taking the class. She said that this did not give me or the school the right to expose him to this.

She is VERY upset, and may be coming to school today to talk to you.

Should I have gotten special permission? What should I do now????

Linda Alberta

11/16/xx

Mr. Berry,

I received a phone call yesterday after you left to go to the game. Since I knew that I would be out tomorrow, I thought I had better leave you a note.

A sheriff's deputy called and said that three of our students, all soccer players, had been arrested the night before for shoplifting. All three boys had been taken to the station, questioned, then released to their parents' custody. He was not sure whether or not the boys would be prosecuted.

As far as I know, Coach Jenkins does not know about this. As you know, the soccer team has a game 11/17 against Lincoln. I went down to talk to him when I got the call, but he was giving the team a pep talk about the Lincoln game, and was talking about this game deciding the conference championship, so I did not want to interrupt him.

I don't know if this affects anything at school, but I wanted you to know. I'll be home from my tests at the hospital by 3 o'clock if you need to talk to me tomorrow.

The deputy was Mary Shew, and the station's number is 745-5000, but she said that she is off duty tomorrow.

Good luck!

Betty

MR. BERRY,

I FOUND THIS NOTE IN THE HALLWAY AFTER THIRD HOUR, AND DIDN'T KNOW WHAT TO DO WITH IT. TOM STILES

John,

Hey, Babe! Guess what? I might be starting the game tonight. Not playing in it, but STARTING in it. If I do that will be scary!

So Babe, should I get "the present" from Susan or not? Its up to you, I don't care.

Can you believe we have been together for 1 year 1 month and 10 days. That's Kool! We've been in love for that long. I know you love me, but are you still in love with me? I am still in love with you and probly will be 4ever (unless you're a jerk).

Let's get together tonight at my house. My parents are not home, and I can show you how much I really love you.

Yours 4ever,

Jessica

December 3, xxxx

Michelle Selma
28952 Washington
Right City, MO 63333

Dear Mr. Berry:

I am writing you to tell you about a situation that is taking place with my daughter Sara in Mrs. Lee's class.

As you may know, my daughter is disabled. She has been diagnosed as having a behavioral problem, and has had an IEP for the past six years.

The problem is that Sara keeps getting into trouble in Mrs. Lee's class. Sara says that she is never sent to the office, but she continues to receive detentions for silly things like talking, eating in class, and getting up out of her seat. I think that the problem is that Mrs. Lee really does not like Sara.

I would like to come to school and sit in on Sara's classes with Mrs. Lee for a few days to see for myself what is happening. I know that I need permission to do this.

Please give me a call at 745-9189 as soon as possible so I can arrange for my visit.

Sincerely,

Michelle Selma

Michelle Selma

SCENARIOS

The items in this chapter are typical of the types of issues that middle school, junior high school, and high school administrators deal with on a daily basis. In using these Scenarios, for whatever purpose, the respondent is to assume the role of John S. Berry. Mr. Berry is the new principal of Washington Middle/Junior High/High School. He was hired as an administrator for this school year, and he started his position in mid-summer. Mr. Berry is referred to in many of the Scenarios.

These items are not intended to be of an in-depth case study nature. Rather, taken as a group, they are meant to represent the diversity of situations a secondary school administrator faces on a daily basis about which he or she must make decisions. Some Scenarios are simple and require rather simple solutions. Others take more thought and may even lead the reader to ask questions about the situation that cannot be answered from the information in the Scenario that has been presented.

Several Scenarios are written in two formats—a Basic format and an Advanced format. You will see this noted in the Scenario title. A Basic Scenario presents a rather simple problem or situation. In the Advanced version of the same Scenario, the problem or situation is expanded and more complex.

The Scenarios should cause the reader to reflect on how he or she would respond to the situations. A major component of each response is formulating the questions for which answers must be found before a response is given. Through a process of reflection, application of prior academic training, and experience, the reader will be able to ask the appropriate questions and give the "correct" responses to these hypothetical items. Through this process, the reader will be better equipped to handle similar situations in the real world of secondary school administration.

To help users begin to ask the proper questions on their own, Discussion Starter Questions can be found in Chapter 4. These questions may be used in a variety of ways but are especially helpful in the beginning stages of aspiring administrator training programs.

Scenario #1

IT'S A HIT!

Tamika Krother arrives at the school nurse's office at the beginning of the school day, crying and complaining that her arm hurts. When you question her about how her injury occurred, she replies that she was hit by the mirror of a car as the car drove by. According to Tamika, the impact was hard enough that it knocked the mirror off the car.

When you question Tamika further about the incident, you find that the incident happened this morning as she was waiting for her bus. A high school student who attends a neighboring high school and who lives in Tamika's neighborhood drove the car. Tamika says that the car appeared to be heading for her and that as she moved closer to the edge of the road, the car continued to head for her.

When asked whether the driver of the car even knew he had hit her, Tamika said he did because he stopped to ask whether she was all right. Tamika replied to the driver that she was fine.

Scenario #2

WORDS WILL EVER HURT ME

Gina Tracy comes to your office to say that other girls are threatening to beat her up and are calling her vulgar names. It seems that the root of the problem is the recent romance of Gina and her boyfriend, Dan Yates. Dan had broken up with his previous girlfriend last week, and this ex-girlfriend and her friends are the ones who have said threatening and unkind things to Gina. Gina knows the names of some of the girls, but not all of them.

On further discussion, you offer to mediate the situation between Gina and the other girls. Gina responds that she doesn't want the situation to be mediated because the fact that she told anyone in the school what has been happening would only result in worse harassment. She wants nothing to be done. Gina says she only came to you so that you would know what had been happening.

Even though you do not agree with Gina, you call her mother to find out her opinion. Gina's mother also says she does not want Gina to be involved in mediation, does not want the other girls to be called to the office to be questioned, and does not want the other girls' parents to be contacted. Her feeling is that if the entire situation is ignored, it will "blow over" with time.

Scenario #3

FAN-ATICAL
(BASIC)

You are supervising at a freshman boys' basketball away game early in the season. You are watching the game in the third quarter, popcorn and soda in hand, when one of the referees stops the game and asks whether an administrator from your school is in attendance. You quickly dump your snacks in the trash can, head out onto the floor, and tell the referee who you are.

The referee quickly turns toward where most of the fans from your school are sitting, points to a man (the father of one of the players), and asks you to talk to him about constantly harassing the referees. The referee also wants this man to leave the gym. Because you did not hear anything the man said, you ask the referee what the man has been saying. The referee answers that he has been yelling "derogatory stuff." You ask whether the man has been cursing at him. The referee responds that he has heard no curse words.

As you go over to talk with the parent in the stands, the basketball game resumes.

Scenario #4

FAN-ATICAL
(ADVANCED)

You are supervising at a freshman boys' basketball away game early in the season. You are watching the game in the third quarter, popcorn and soda in hand, when one of the referees stops the game and asks whether an administrator from your school is in attendance. You quickly dump your snacks in the trash can, head out onto the floor, and tell the referee who you are.

The referee quickly turns toward where most of the fans from your school are sitting, points to a man (the father of one of the players), and asks you to talk to him about constantly harassing the referees. The referee also wants this man to leave the gym. Because you did not hear what the man said, you ask the referee what the man has been saying. The referee answers that he has been yelling "derogatory stuff." You ask whether the man has been cursing at him. The referee responds that he has heard no curse words.

As you go over to talk with the parent in the stands, the basketball game resumes. When you reach the parent, Mr. Roelker, you shake his hand and introduce yourself. Mr. Roelker seems calm and polite. You ask him whether he has been saying things to the referees, and he indicates that he has. Mr. Roelker goes on to tell you about what a poor job the officials are doing of officiating.

Next, you tell Mr. Roelker that the referee has asked that he leave the gym. Mr. Roelker again tells you what a poor job the officials are doing. He tells you that his oldest son is an official, that he has watched him work with many other referees, and that the two who are officiating at the game tonight are the worst he has ever seen. You explain to him that whether or not he disagrees with the calls, he cannot badger the officials. He lowers his chin, nods, and says, "Yeah, I know."

Mr. Roelker asks whether he has to leave the building. You tell him he only needs to leave the gym, which he now does promptly. Mr. Roelker stands just outside the gym entrance, in the foyer, watching as much of the game as he can. He is now well out of earshot of both referees.

You believe that everything is under control for the time being. You are concerned about what will happen after the game, when the officials head to their locker room via a route that will be relatively near Mr. Roelker.

As the final buzzer sounds, you station yourself between where Mr. Roelker is and where the officials will be. He says nothing, and you are relieved. You would like to have the full story of what the referee who complained about Mr. Roelker heard, so you ask the principal of the host school if you can talk to the officials. He says you may and takes you to the officials' locker room.

In the locker room, the officials are sipping soft drinks and relaxing before showering. The principal introduces you to the referees. The referee who complained about Mr. Roelker is willing to speak with you about the incident and begins to tell you what he heard.

At about this time, there is a knock on the door, and the other official opens it. At the open door stands a woman who begins to "tell off" the official you're speaking with by complaining about what he did to her husband. When she sees you, she quickly walks away before you have a chance to say anything.

You finish your conversation with the referee. You find that Mr. Roelker had been making such comments as "You stink," "They should pull your official's license," "This isn't grade school," and "My grandma could do better." The referee indicates that no profanity had been used. By the time you leave the locker room, Mr. and Mrs. Roelker have left for home.

The next morning, you receive a call from Mr. Roelker. He wants to meet with you this afternoon. He apologizes for his behavior. Your calendar has a slot open in the early afternoon, and you agree to meet with him.

When you meet with Mr. Roelker, you discuss with him such things as sportsmanship and being a role model for the students/athletes. He says that he understands his behavior was wrong but that he is really here to talk about the poor officiating. You explain that officials do their best but might occasionally make a poor call. You also say that there is a proper means by which truly bad officials can be reported to the governing association, and you explain this procedure to Mr. Roelker. Mr. Roelker listens when you tell him that poor officiating needs to be reported in this manner, as opposed to individuals harassing referees. He agrees but says that, in regard to last night's situation, he will "let it go."

Before you end your meeting, you mention to Mr. Roelker that it was highly improper for his wife to come to the referees' locker room to "chew them out." When you mention this, Mr. Roelker looks puzzled. It is then clear to you that he did not know this had happened. He says he will talk to his wife about this.

At the next freshman boys' basketball game, another away game, you make sure you are not seated until the fans have taken their seats. For obvious reasons, you find Mr. Roelker in the crowd and then choose a seat approximately between him and the basketball court. This game has a different set of referees, and you are glad for this.

During the first half, you hear no comments from Mr. Roelker, but as the competition begins to heat up in the second half, you begin to hear things being said about the officiating that are obviously not loud enough for the officials to hear. Then a controversial foul is called, and you hear Mr. Roelker call out, "You meathead," as play resumes and the official passes by on his way back down the court.

Scenario #5

ROOM FOR A CHANGE

Jim Robles has been a teacher in your building for the past 17 years. He is well respected by some of his peers but is seen as being a complainer by others.

This year, Jim was assigned a classroom he has been unhappy with since the beginning of the year. Jim comes to you in October and complains about the stairs he has to climb to get to this classroom. He says, without written medical evidence, that he has a rare bone problem that causes pain in his knees when he climbs stairs and that it is an undue hardship on him to have to teach in a classroom he has to climb stairs to get to.

Jim further points out to you that a new science teacher has gotten a more desirable room and that he would like to have that room for the next semester. You explain that the new teacher has this room to be close to her mentor, which is very important in your estimation, and that his chance of being assigned that room any time this year is very slim. Jim does not accept this answer and comments that you are just trying to "push him out." He also comments to you that, in his mind, this issue is worth fighting for "through the proper channels."

Scenario #6

HAIR TODAY, GONE TOMORROW

Stephanie Taley, a teacher in your building, comes to you and says that her aide, Tom Stiles, left the building for his 15-minute break and did not come back on time. Furthermore, when Tom finally did return from his break, it was obvious that his hair had been professionally cut.

You ask Tom to meet with you after school, which he does. When you ask Tom whether he left the building during his break time to get a haircut, he says that he can do anything he wants to do on his break. You agree that, to an extent, this is true, but you still question whether he left the building during his break to get a haircut. Tom replies, "My break is my time, and I can do what I want. Even if I did get a haircut, I was back in 15 minutes." You question the physical possibility of this even though you know there is a barbershop just down the street.

Your final response to Tom is that he must notify you from now on when he leaves the building for any reason. In fact, this will become a requirement for all teacher aides. You also tell Tom to make sure his breaks last no longer that 15 minutes and that if he does not adhere to this, the problem will be documented. You tell him that this documentation would be put in his file and could be used as evidence for not rehiring him next year.

Tom's final response to you is that he would like to have a meeting with you after school one day next week. Tom wants his lawyer present at this meeting and would like you to tell the lawyer what you have just told him!

Scenario #7

FIX THE PROBLEM
(BASIC)

Michael Printz is a student in your building whose learning disability qualifies him to be educated under the Individuals With Disabilities Education Act (IDEA). Michael has an Individualized Education Plan (IEP) in place. After first-quarter report cards come out, you receive a call from Michael's mother, Susan Theim. Ms. Theim indicates to you that Michael has failed all but two of his classes for the first quarter and that she is very concerned about this. Ms. Theim respectfully requests a meeting with you and the Special Education Department chairperson. You agree and set up the meeting for 2 days from now. You also review Michael's IEP in preparation for the meeting.

Ms. Theim shows up on time to the meeting. With her is a person she identifies as Mary Glore, an advocate with the local child advocacy agency. You introduce yourself and Mrs. Susan Lee, Special Education Department Chairperson in your building.

You begin the meeting by reviewing Michael's grades from first quarter. Mrs. Lee has also obtained current reports from each of Michael's teachers, which she wishes to review at the meeting. These are the only pieces of information you have about Michael, as this is the first time his case has been brought to your attention.

Before you and Mrs. Lee can proceed with your unofficial agenda for the meeting, Mrs. Glore speaks up and says, in essence, that they are really here to address Michael's disability and how special accommodations written within his IEP are not being implemented by Michael's teachers. Ms. Theim and Mrs. Glore both want to know why the accommodations have not been made and what you are going to do to "fix" Michael's first-quarter grades.

Scenario #8

FIX THE PROBLEM
(ADVANCED)

Michael Printz is a student in your building whose learning disability qualifies him to be educated under the Individuals With Disabilities Education Act (IDEA). Michael has an Individualized Education Plan (IEP) in place. After first-quarter report cards come out, you receive a call from Michael's mother, Susan Theim. Ms. Theim indicates to you that Michael has failed all but two of his classes for the first quarter and that she is very concerned about this. Ms. Theim respectfully requests a meeting with you and the Special Education Department chairperson. You agree and set up the meeting for 2 days from now. You also review Michael's IEP in preparation for the meeting. You notice that a variety of accommodations within Michael's IEP must be made.

Ms. Theim shows up on time to the meeting. With her is a person she identifies as Mary Glore, an advocate with the local child advocacy agency. You introduce yourself and Mrs. Susan Lee, Special Education Department Chairperson in your building.

You begin the meeting by reviewing Michael's grades from first quarter. Mrs. Lee has also obtained current reports from each of Michael's teachers, which she wishes to review at the meeting. These are the only pieces of information you have about Michael, as this is the first time his case has been brought to your attention.

Before you and Mrs. Lee can proceed with your unofficial agenda for the meeting, Mrs. Glore speaks up and says, in essence, that they are really here to address Michael's disability and how special accommodations written within his IEP are not being implemented by Michael's teachers. Ms. Theim and Mrs. Glore both want to know why the accommodations have not been made and what you are going to do to "fix" Michael's first-quarter grades.

You ask exactly how they perceive that accommodations explained within Michael's IEP are not being made. Mrs. Glore says that Michael's IEP states that he is to receive extended time to complete assignments and that this time is not being given to him. She says that Ms. Theim has talked with Michael's teachers and that each one, with the exception of his social studies teacher, has indicated that if he had turned in more of his work he would have passed the class.

You explain that you will have to gather more information from the teachers before any decision can be made regarding Michael. You acknowledge that the IEP does call for extended time to turn in work but that you were not aware of any problems with this until it had just now been brought to your attention.

You next ask exactly what the women meant by the earlier statement that the student's first-quarter grades need to be "fixed." Mrs. Glore again speaks up and says that Michael should be excused from any assignments he was not given extended time to complete and that his grades should be recalculated as if these assignments had never been assigned. You respond that you are not sure this can be done but that you are willing to look into the situation and then decide how to proceed. You and Mrs. Lee shake hands with both of the women, and you promise to give them a call as soon as you can gather more information, probably in about 2 days. You then escort them to the front door of the school.

After the two women have left, you and Mrs. Lee discuss the situation. You get out Michael's IEP and review it. Just as you had remembered, one item spelled out in this document is that Michael is to get extended time on assignments, but it does not specify how much extra time should be given. You and Mrs. Lee decide that you need to talk with Michael's teachers about his progress in their classes. You ask your secretary to schedule an emergency meeting with Michael's teachers tomorrow morning.

At the meeting with the teachers, you are most concerned with whether they knew that Michael was to receive extensions on assignment deadlines and whether extensions had been granted. All his teachers, with the exception of his art teacher, knew of this accommodation and said they had, in fact, granted Michael extended time to turn in his assignments. Michael had received a B in art for the quarter.

When you ask exactly how long assignments have been extended, the answers the teachers give are varied. They range from 2 weeks to all the way to the end of the quarter. The majority of the teachers also indicate that they had contacted Ms. Theim on numerous occasions and had told her about the missing work. According to the teachers, her response was always that she would talk with Michael and would tell him that he needed to do the work and turn it in immediately. The teachers also indicate that, on the basis of test grades in their classes, Michael was at least a C student but that he seemed to be lazy about turning things in.

It seems to you that the teachers have met their obligations in extending time to Michael on his assignments. You do recognize, however, that the IEP does not specify what the time extension should be and that this might be a "loophole" you will have to deal with. You do not think it is fair to allow all missed assignments to be excused.

You decide to call Ms. Theim and tell her about your findings. She is not home when you call, so you leave a message on her answering machine. About an hour later, Mary Glore, from the local child advocacy agency, calls. You tell her about what you found out in your meeting with the teachers. You also tell her that you are not comfortable excusing all the missed assignments. Mrs. Glore is not happy with this and indicates such to you. She states that you and the teachers are just trying to cover up for not doing your jobs, and she demands another meeting by the end of this week to bring this problem to a conclusion. She says that Ms. Theim is ready to take immediate steps to remedy the problem in another way if you and the teachers are not ready to admit your mistake. You kindly agree to meet with her and Mrs. Theim in the morning 2 days from now.

Scenario #9

I HAVE A GREAT JOB!

One of your teachers is having a Career Day in her classroom only, which you are aware of. Her method for obtaining speakers is to ask each student whether a parent could come to speak about his or her career. Many great speakers have been obtained by using this method.

When one particular student, Ryan Tates, was asked what his parent might speak about, Ryan told his teacher that his father was a salesman and that he wanted to talk to the class about all the aspects of sales—from obtaining new customers to servicing customers after the sale. When Ryan was asked whom his father worked for, he replied that his father sold beer for Blue Bird Distributing, the local distributor of a popular brand.

On hearing what company Ryan's father worked for, the teacher told Ryan that his father could not be allowed to speak to the class about his job because it involved a product that would be controversial among classmates' parents and that was illegal for minors to buy or consume. Ryan seemed disappointed, but the teacher apologized for having to make the decision.

The next day, you receive a call from Ryan's father, Mr. Tates. He is very upset with Ryan's teacher for having said, in so many words, that his occupation was not an honorable one. He said that Ryan was sorry he had ever volunteered information about his father's occupation, because the teacher's response embarrassed him. In fact, Ryan was kept home from school today because he wasn't sure he could face his classmates. To help his son "save face," Mr. Tates demands that he be allowed to speak to Ryan's class about his career in sales.

Scenario #10

YOU MAKE THE CALL

Ron Jenkins teaches physical education in your school, and he is also the varsity basketball and soccer coach. Coach Jenkins is known for his no-nonsense style of doing things, and he is recognized as an excellent teacher who expects much of his physical education students. He is a tough coach, too, but he is respected by his athletes and their parents.

One day, you receive a telephone call from the mother of Kamal Haddad, a physical education student of Coach Jenkins. The parent complains to you about the way Coach Jenkins spoke to her son yesterday in class. When you ask about specifics, Kamal's mother tells you that, according to her son, the boys in the class were flipping each other with towels in the locker room. Then, suddenly, Coach Jenkins started yelling at them and told them they were all retarded and belonged in the psychiatric ward at the local hospital. Mrs. Haddad wants Coach Jenkins to be disciplined and wants both her and the school district's superintendent to be informed of your response to this situation.

You tell Mrs. Haddad that your first step will be to talk with Coach Jenkins, and she agrees that this is a proper way to begin to respond to the problem. In talking with Coach Jenkins, you find out that he had given the boys repeated warnings that day to stop flipping towels before someone got seriously hurt and that the boys continued to ignore his warnings. Kamal, according to Coach Jenkins, was "the biggest duck in the puddle" in the towel-flipping incident. It seems that every time the flipping would begin to die down, Kamal would start another round. When questioned about what he had said, Coach Jenkins said he had been very angry and did not remember the exact words he had used. He did, however, remember saying something about them being retarded if they did not understand what he had told them the first time.

Scenario #11
BALANCING ACT

A math teacher, Mrs. Suarez, comes to you on January 21, the second day of the second semester, with a complaint. Mrs. Suarez states that she has an average of 31 students in her algebra classes for the semester and that the class average for the other algebra teacher in the building in only 28. Mrs. Suarez explains that the difference in average of three students does not seem like much but that when you multiply that by seven classes, it equates to 21 more students than the other algebra teacher. This, she explains, is almost equal to teaching another class because of the number of papers that have to be hand-graded in a class like algebra.

Mrs. Suarez demands that an adjustment be made in the number of students she has in her classes to make her average the same as the other algebra teacher's. Although Mrs. Suarez is pleasant in her demands, she says that if the changes are not made, she will file a grievance with the local teachers' union.

Scenario #12
TOO HOT TO HANDLE

Just after the buses have pulled away, one bus pulls back into the school parking lot. You go to investigate and find that a student has been verbally abusing the bus driver by calling her vulgar names and by making vulgar gestures to her. The student admits this but says that the bus driver provoked him. The bus driver states that she will not take this child home today because his behavior is so distracting to her that she believes she cannot transport him and the other students safely. You take the student off the bus, send the bus driver with her full load of students on her way, and take the student into the school office.

You are able to contact the student's mother at work, and you explain to her the situation. You also tell the student's mother that she will have to pick him up and that you will wait with the student in the office until she arrives. The student's mother agrees to come immediately to pick up her son and then asks to speak with him on the telephone. You comply with this request and are called out of the office to handle another situation just as you hand the student the telephone.

Within about 15 minutes, the student's mother arrives. She immediately introduces herself and explains that she is not a very nice person and has been known to "cuss out" a principal. She then tells you that her son has been treated unfairly and that if she does not get some answers, she will go to her friend on the school board to let her know how she feels.

Scenario #13

DRUG STORE (BASIC)

Connie Able, a gifted student who has been on the honor roll every semester she has been at your school, comes to your office and asks to talk with you. You invite her in. She closes the door as she enters your office and then begins to tell you about a student who she believes is selling marijuana at school.

You ask Connie why she suspects this. Connie tells you she saw Stacey Pennant and Lisa Zerano exchanging money for a little bag in the girls' rest room. As far as she was concerned, Stacey now had drug money in her possession, and Lisa had the "stuff."

You have always suspected Lisa as someone who may be using drugs, although you have never received any information like this. Lisa has never been in trouble in or out of school for issues related to drugs. She has, however, been in trouble at school for truancy, classroom disruptions, and smoking on campus.

You do not know Stacey, and when you check her discipline file, you find that she has no prior discipline referrals.

Connie pleads that you *please* not let these girls know she told you anything.

Scenario #14

DRUG STORE
(ADVANCED)

Connie Able, a gifted students who has been on the honor roll every semester she has been at your school, comes to your office and asks to talk with you. You invite her in. She closes the door as she enters your office and then begins to tell you about a student who she believes is selling marijuana at school.

You ask Connie why she suspects this. Connie tells you she saw Stacey Pennant and Lisa Zerano exchanging money for a little bag in the girls' rest room. As far as she was concerned, Stacey now had drug money in her possession, and Lisa had the "stuff."

You have always suspected Lisa as someone who may be using drugs, although you have never received any information like this. Lisa has never been in trouble in or out of school for issues related to drugs. She has, however, been in trouble at school for truancy, classroom disruptions, and smoking on campus.

You do not know Stacey, and when you check her discipline file, you find that she has no prior discipline referrals.

Connie pleads that you *please* not let these girls know she told you anything.

At this point, you plan to call each "suspect" into your office to talk with her about the information you have received because you believe that you have enough evidence to at least ask some questions. You want to talk with each girl separately to see what each has to say.

You go to Lisa's class to bring her to your office. After both of you arrive in your office, you ask Lisa about the exchange that was reported to you, and she denies knowing what you're talking about. When you ask whether she has any contraband on her or in her locker, she says no with a smug look on her face. You then escort Lisa to her academic counselor's office. You explain to Lisa and her counselor that she is to stay there until you come back for her. You suggest that they discuss Lisa's poor grades and begin planning how she can bring them up.

Next, you go to Stacey Pennant's classroom and escort her to your office. Stacey looks nervous from the outset, and when you ask her about this morning's alleged deal, she readily tells you about it. Stacey says she is very frightened that if she does not tell the truth she will be in more trouble and will have to go to jail.

Stacey says she was the "go between" for a dealer outside school. She says the dealer told her that if she did not work for him, he would hurt her and her family. You ask for more details about the supplier and the deal, and Stacey readily gives you all the facts.

When you ask Stacey whether she has any more drugs at school, she says no. She also tells you that Lisa's drugs are no longer in the school building because Lisa had managed to sneak to her car and hide them there. Lisa had told Stacey something about the car being off limits to searches because it was private property and not even the police could touch it without a warrant and that, by the time that happened, she would be "feelin' good."

Scenario #15
OUT-OF-TOWN GUEST

A nicely dressed professional woman arrives at your office and tells your secretary she is the parent of Justin Neman. She then introduces herself to you as Sherry Grimes and explains that she lives out of town but happens to be in town today on important personal business. She says she has decided to stop by to find out about her son.

Justin, she says, has lived here with his natural father (her ex-husband) for about a year, and she has had little contact with Justin or his natural father since that time. Until last year, Justin had lived with her and her second husband, Jerry Grimes.

This very articulate and pleasant woman asks to see Justin's academic records (copies of all report cards and progress reports), discipline records, and attendance records.

Scenario #16

IN THE MONEY NOW

You are in charge of the budget in your building. One day, you receive a bank statement from State Bank with Joan Smith's name, the school's name, and the school's address on it. You have not seen such a statement during the time you have been principal in this building, and you wonder about the nature of the statement.

As you begin to investigate, you first talk with the secretary who sorts the mail. She tells you that she receives such a statement every month but that she forwards it directly to Ms. Smith because the statement has her name on it. The secretary explains that you must have received this month's statement because a substitute secretary sorted the mail yesterday, and this secretary had been told that anything that had to do with finances should be routed to you.

Your next step is to speak with Joan Smith. Ms. Smith tells you that she opened this account in her name and the school's name about 5 years ago. She uses this account to handle student fund-raisers that she does in the school for the many organizations she is involved in. She personally makes all deposits and writes all checks. When you ask how much money is currently in this account, Ms. Smith tells you that this statement shows a balance of $5,119.36. When asked whether the former principal had authorized this account being set up, Ms. Smith indicates that he had not.

Scenario #17

LOOKIN' MIGHTY GOOD

A female student comes into your office and says that she wants to speak with you. You invite her in and ask how you can help her. She appears to be very nervous but begins to tell you about a boy in her class who is saying "nasty" things to her that make her feel uncomfortable. You stop the girl at that point and call for a female counselor to hear this complaint with you.

When the counselor arrives, you explain to the student why you have invited the counselor (because this is a potential sexual harassment issue and your district recommends that a team approach be used in handling such cases). The student understands and is agreeable in telling both of you what the problem is.

The student explains that a boy in one of her classes looks at her and says to her, "Hey, you're lookin' mighty good today," to her on almost a daily basis. This always happens when the teacher is not aware of what is going on. The girl goes on to explain that she has asked the boy to stop because the statement makes her feel uncomfortable, but this has been going on for about a month now and he will not stop. This is the first time she has let anyone in the school know about this situation, and she has not told her parents about it.

Scenario #18

PICKING ON ME
(BASIC)

During the first 3 weeks of school, Steve Stone, a ninth-grade student, is sent to your office. You find that Steve has a discipline referral in his hand from the teacher who sent him to you. Ms. Danielle Potter, his math teacher, is the referring teacher.

The discipline notice reads that Steve has been disruptive in class by talking out and that he will not respond to correction.

You ask Steve what happened in the class. Steve tells you that the teacher was just "picking on him." You respond that this would be unlike the teacher and that there must have been more to the situation than that. Steve responds by saying, "F_ _ _ you, I ain't going to sit here and listen to your bull_ _ _ _." Steve then gets up and walks out.

Scenario #19

PICKING ON ME (ADVANCED)

During the first 3 weeks of school, Steve Stone, a ninth-grade student, is sent to your office. You find that Steve has a discipline referral in his hand from the teacher who sent him to you. Ms. Danielle Potter, his math teacher, is the referring teacher. You have not seen Steve in your office before.

The discipline notice reads that Steve has been disruptive in class by talking out and that he will not respond to correction.

You ask Steve what happened in the class. Steve tells you that the teacher was just "picking on him." You respond that this would be unlike the teacher and that there must have been more to the situation than that. Steve responds by saying, "F_ _ _ you, I ain't going to sit here and listen to your bull_ _ _ _." Steve then gets up and walks out.

You follow Steve and tell him to stop and come back to your office. Steve pays no attention to you, does not stop, and does not respond to you in any way. You continue to follow Steve and ask him again to stop. He still does not do what you ask of him.

At this point, you catch up to Steve and step in front of him. He says, "Get out of my face," and begins to step around you. You step in front of him, and he says, "I said, get out of my d_ _ _ face," and again tries to step around you. When you step in front of him again, he turns around and starts walking the opposite way.

You again tell Steve to stop, and you ask him where he is going. He finally responds by saying that he is leaving this school and is never coming back. You tell him that if he leaves, he will be truant. He responds that he doesn't care and that you will be sorry if you try to stop him.

As you continue to follow Steve, he finally does leave the building and walks across the parking lot and into the adjoining neighborhood until you cannot see him.

You immediately go to your office to try to find out some information on Steve, including a telephone number at which to contact Steve's parents. When looking into his record, you discover that Steve is 14 years of age. You also find out that this is the first year he has been a student in your school district. He transferred to your school from a neighboring community and enrolled just before school started.

As a result of finding out Steve's age, you call the local police to let them know a student walked out of your school. You tell them what you know, and they respond that they will keep a look out for him and will contact you if they see him.

In the file, you find Steve's registration papers, which include telephone numbers at which his father can be reached. It is apparent from these papers that Steve lives with his father, as his mother is not listed on any of the paperwork and has signed nothing. Documents in the file indicate that Steve's parents have joint custody of him.

You call Mr. Stone at work. After you introduce yourself, you tell him of the situation, including the fact that Steve has left school and that you have called the police. Mr. Stone tells you that he had hoped nothing like this would happen but is not surprised.

As you continue to speak with Mr. Stone, he explains that he and his ex-wife were divorced when Steve was 2 years old and that Steve has only been living with him for about a month. The reason Steve came to live with him is that his mother is dying of cancer. She has been sick for about a year but has gotten progressively worse over that past 6 weeks. It became obvious that she could not care for Steve because she was in and out of the hospital and was sometimes admitted for several days at a time.

Mr. Stone says that Steve asked this morning whether he could stay home from school today because he had a feeling this would be the day his mother would die and that he wanted to be by her side when it happened. He tells you he explained to Steve that his mother had been this sick before and that she was not likely to get any worse today. He had also told Steve that if he got any word about his mother's condition getting worse, he would contact him at school. Before Mr. Stone went to work, he had made sure that Steve had gotten on the bus.

Steve was not happy this morning with his father's decision, and according to Mr. Stone, his son is not terribly happy about living with him. Mr. Stone tells you there were some legitimate circumstances why he and Steve's mother were divorced and why he did not see his son very often for several years. He says that

Steve does not understand any of this and is bitter about him having left Steve and his mother.

As to an immediate solution to the problem, Mr. Stone says that he will leave work and drive over to the neighborhood where Steve was last seen and look for him. Mr. Stone says he'll bring Steve back to school if he finds him.

Scenario #20
NUMBER, PLEASE

You receive a call from your local law enforcement agency. The officer tells you he has picked up Michelle Kim, one of your students, who is 14 years of age. Michelle was found during school hours, driving her mother's car down Main Street.

You have met Michelle's mother, Suong Kim, on several occasions and have a good working relationship with her when it comes to dealing with Michelle. Michelle's mother is very supportive of the school and is always pleasant in talking about solutions to problems. She respects you and most often agrees with your opinion of how to handle Michelle.

The officer asks you for a telephone number so that he can contact Michelle's parents. He wants to call them so that they can pick her up at the police station and also pick up the car and drive it home.

Scenario #21
STUDENT AIDS

You are sitting in your office one morning when the telephone rings. Your secretary answers it and tells you a parent on the line wants to speak with you.

When you pick up the receiver, you find out that the person calling is the mother of one of your male students who has physical education during 5th hour this semester. The mother, who will not identify herself, claims that she knows that another male student in her son's 5th-hour physical education class has AIDS. She tells you she wants this student out of her son's class immediately and identifies to you the student who she claims has the illness.

Scenario #22
a, b, c, D, e, F...

You meet with Wanda Masterson, a math teacher in your building, to discuss her regular performance evaluation for the year. During your October 15 meeting, as part of your regular process, you examine Ms. Masterson's grade book. You notice that, on the past two major tests, more than 50% of the students received a grade of D or F.

This many low grades on tests seems out of the ordinary to you, and you ask Ms. Masterson why this might happen and how it can be addressed. You also ask how students could go on to the next topic or unit without having mastered the current materials.

Ms. Masterson's response to your questions is that she has so much curriculum to cover that she does not have time to reteach when the majority of students receive Ds or Fs. Ms. Masterson goes on to state that she teaches the material but has no guarantee the students will learn it. She thinks their lack of effort during the unit is what finally becomes evident on tests.

Scenario #23
ALARMED
(BASIC)

One morning, shortly after school has started and all the students are in their classes, you are sitting at the desk in your office, reading the mail that arrived on your desk at the end of the previous day. A student walks in and hands you a note, indicating it is from his math teacher, Mrs. Throm. He says Mrs. Throm has asked that you read the note right away.

You open the note and are alarmed to find that Mrs. Throm has overheard two students in her current class talking about a gun they think a third student has in his book bag. In her note, Mrs. Throm asks for your immediate assistance.

Scenario #24

ALARMED (ADVANCED)

One morning, shortly after school has started and all the students are in their classes, you are sitting at the desk in your office, reading the mail that arrived on your desk at the end of the previous day. A student walks in and hands you a note, indicating it is from his math teacher, Mrs. Throm. He says Mrs. Throm has asked that you read the note right away.

You open the note and are alarmed to find that Mrs. Throm has overheard two students in her current class talking about a gun they think a third student has in his book bag. In her note, Mrs. Throm asks for your immediate assistance.

You go to Mrs. Throm's room immediately and ask her to step into the hallway where both of you can monitor her class yet speak somewhat privately. Mrs. Throm seems relieved that you are there. You ask her what she has heard, and she indicates that what she heard was basically what she had indicated in her note to you. You ask whether the name of the student who may have the gun was mentioned, and she says it was not. Mrs. Throm then gives you the names of the students who were talking, and you step into the class and ask for them to come with you to the office. It is now about halfway through 1st hour, which is 55 minutes in length.

When you arrive at your office, you take the students in and shut the door. Both students are male. When asked, one boy identifies himself as Julian Boles, and the other boy identifies himself as Mike Mound. You know neither of these boys because you have never seen them in your office, but you do recognize their faces.

You immediately tell Julian and Mike why they are here and then ask them why they believe that another student may have a gun. In almost the same breath, you ask them who this other student is. They identify the student who may have a gun as Matthew David. You recognize this name but recollect that this student is a rather quiet young man who sits alone at lunch most of the time.

Julian then says that when they were sitting in the cafeteria this morning just before school started, some bigger boys seemed to be picking on Matthew. While Julian was sitting across the way from where this incident happened, his perception was that the bigger boys were talking to Matthew to try to "shake him down" for something. Julian tells you that he later heard Matthew say something about a gun.

Without asking any further questions, you think that, at this point, you have a picture in your mind of what has happened. You surmise that a smaller boy has been being picked on and that he finally has gotten tired of it and has brought a weapon to school to take care of the problem.

You immediately ask your secretary to make an announcement that all students are to stay in their classes until the teachers are instructed to release them. Also, all teachers are instructed to give no one a hall pass to go anywhere. You instruct the teachers to contact the office via the intercom if they have any questions. You next call the police and tell them the situation at hand. The dispatcher replies that he is sending several officers to the school immediately.

You then turn your attention back to Julian and Mike, and you ask them what else they know about the situation. Mike tells you that, in the cafeteria this morning, the bigger boys finally walked away from Matthew. By then, he and Julian were walking toward Matthew and they saw him reach into his book bag and heard him mutter the words "I got the gun right here."

At about this time, a call comes into the office over the intercom from one of the classrooms. When your secretary answers the call, a teacher asks whether it is all right to let a student go to the nurse because the teacher thinks the student might be sick. You hear the request and tell your secretary to ask the teacher who the student is. She replies that it is Matthew David. You tell your secretary to instruct the teacher not to let the student go and that you will be there as fast as you can. You take off literally running to the classroom.

The classroom is very close to the office, and you arrive there quickly. You cautiously peer into the classroom so as not to be seen by Matthew. Matthew is sitting in a desk, with his head down, and his book bag is on the floor by him. You are now faced with a dilemma. The police have not arrived yet, the book bag where the gun allegedly may be is lying on the floor, and the student's head is down on the desk. This seems to you to be an opportune time to rush in and seize the boy, but you are not sure quite how to do so.

Fortunately, as you are pausing a moment (which seems like hours) to make up your mind, three police officers come walking around the corner.

One officer introduces himself as Tyrell Marsh and asks what details you know about the situation. You tell him what you know, and he peers in at the boy. The officer evaluates the situation and then develops a plan based on the size of the boy, where he is located, and the fact that he appears to be sleeping. The plan is to have one officer "cover" at gunpoint while the other two officers approach the boy and escort him out of the room.

The plan is immediately enacted, and the rather small and frightened-looking boy is soon in your office. Once inside your office, you explain to Matthew about the report that he stated he had a gun in his book bag and that other students had heard this statement. Matthew begins to stammer that he does not know what you are talking about, and at the same time one of the officers is looking through Matthew's book bag. As you tell Matthew that he will only be in more trouble if he lies, his pockets are checked by another police officer. At about this time, the entire contents of the book bag are placed on your desk. Stacked there are several books, some notebooks, several sheets of loose paper, two pencils, one pen, and a large package of GUM!

You find nothing else on or with Matthew, save his lunch money. You reach over and grab the gum. As you do so, a light seems to go on in Matthew's head. Without further questions, Matthew remembers that he had made a comment this morning in the cafeteria about gum. He says that some boys had been asking him for gum but that he told them repeatedly he did not have any he could give them (not a lie in his mind; he thought the gum he did have could not be given away because he would need it himself). After the boys finally walked away, he felt so proud of himself for fending them off, which he often did not do, that he proudly reached into his book bag and declared out loud, "I got the gum right here." This, he says, must have been what some other students heard.

To your amazement, you look at the clock and notice that first period is just about to end. You ask your secretary to announce that all students are to be released according to schedule and that normal procedures are to be resumed. As you finish this request, Matthew asks whether he can go to the nurse to take some of his headache medicine. He states that he has had one of his more minor migraine headaches all morning.

Scenario #25
CAUGHT

Brandon Vincent is a student in your school. He has been found with cigarettes in his possession on two separate occasions this school year and has been disciplined in each of these instances.

On February 16, you call for Brandon to come to your office just after lunch so that you can talk with him about a minor classroom disturbance for which he has been referred. When Brandon enters your office, he smells of cigarette smoke. Because of this and because of his past history, you ask Brandon to empty his pockets. He willing does so, and nothing but small change and a note from his girlfriend are found. You ask Brandon whether he has anything he should not have in his locker. Brandon looks nervous but says no.

You summon a fellow administrator, and both of you go together with Brandon to his locker to look inside. You open the locker with your master key and search it. Inside, tucked away behind a book on the shelf, you find a cigarette package with cigarettes inside.

Brandon has been "busted," and you and your fellow administrator take him back to your office to call his parents and arrange for his discipline. While your partner is lecturing Brandon on the ill effects of smoking, you casually take another look inside the cigarette package and find two marijuana joints mingled among the cigarettes.

You immediately question Brandon about these. He says they are not his. When you ask whose they are and why he has them, he says that they belong to another student and that he is just holding them for the student. You then ask Brandon who this other student is. Brandon responds by telling you he will not "narc" on his friend.

Scenario #26
EMERGENCY

A student arrives at your office, obviously out of breath from running, dressed in physical education attire. The student says that a girl has been injured in physical education class. You ask the student to take you to the injured student, and you follow her to the gym.

When you arrive, you find a female student on the floor, with two physical education teachers attending to her. The remainder of the students from the class are sitting in the bleachers in the gym. Some are visibly upset, some are talking quietly, and some are laughing and enjoying themselves. When you walk over to the student who is lying on the floor, her eyes are open but she is not alert enough to answer simple questions that the physical education teachers have been asking her.

When you ask the teachers what happened, one of them states that the girl fell on her head (on a mat) during a tumbling exercise.

Scenario #27
LOANER

You receive a call on March 12 from Nick Papaganos, the principal of Marble Rock Middle School in your district. Nick says that his school has run out of copier paper and that he has no money left to buy any for the remainder of the year. He asks to borrow 30 cartons of copier paper from your school, which he will pay back when money is available to his school on July 1 of the current year and he can purchase more paper.

From past experience, you believe that you have enough copier paper to make it through the end of the current school year and have about 35 to 40 cartons to spare.

Scenario #28
MISSING FURNITURE

Because of a great increase in students in your district, 12 new classrooms have been added to your building for the upcoming school year. You ordered teacher and student furniture for these rooms in late March, which was well within the time frame the vendor gave you for the furniture to be delivered on time.

Three weeks before school is to start, you still have not received the furniture. You call the vendor and inquire about anticipated delivery date. The vendor tells you the furniture is not scheduled to arrive at your building until 6 weeks from today. You talk to everyone within the vendor's organization, including the president, and the timeline for delivery cannot be changed.

The reason given for the delay is that the summer was so hot at the manufacturing plant in Detroit that the painting operation had to be shut down for 3 weeks.

Scenario #29

NASTY MESS
(BASIC)

One day in October, after the students have left for the day, Jane Seymour, an attractive 30-year-old female custodian, comes to your office with a complaint. You do not know Jane very well because she has only worked in your building for the past 2 weeks. Jane transferred to your building from another school in the district.

Jane complains that a male custodian in your building has been saying "nasty" things to her, has been looking at her "funny," and has made "passes" at her. You ask who the male custodian is, and she says it is David Jones, who has been a custodian in your building for 4 years. David also supervises the night crew, on which both he and Jane work.

You ask Jane whether she feels comfortable telling you more about the specifics of the matter, and she says yes. She says that David has asked her how much she would charge for a nude picture of herself, has asked her out on a date several times, and frequently stares at her and "licks his chops." He has also said that he will make her job miserable if she will not go out with him on a date.

You ask her to write out her complaint and sign it, which she does. As Jane hands you the signed document, she says that she does not want anyone to get into trouble but that she just wants the harassment to stop. You instruct Jane to say nothing about this to David and explain to her that it is important you have a chance to speak with him before he knows of the complaint. You tell her that you will follow up on her complaint as soon as possible and that she is to tell you if anything else occurs before the matter is settled.

Scenario #30

NASTY MESS (ADVANCED)

One day in October, after the students have left for the day, Jane Seymour, an attractive 30-year-old female custodian, comes to your office with a complaint. You do not know Jane very well because she has only worked in your building for the past 2 weeks. Jane transferred to your building from another school in the district.

Jane complains that a male custodian in your building has been saying "nasty" things to her, has been looking at her "funny," and has made "passes" at her. You ask who the male custodian is, and she says it is David Jones, who has been a custodian in your building for 4 years. David also supervises the night crew, on which both he and Jane work.

You ask Jane whether she feels comfortable telling you more about the specifics of the matter, and she says yes. She says that David has asked her how much she would charge for a nude picture of herself, has asked her out on a date several times, and frequently stares at her and "licks his chops." He has also said that he will make her job miserable if she will not go out with him on a date.

You ask her to write out her complaint and sign it, which she does. As Jane hands you the signed document, she says that she does not want anyone to get into trouble but that she just wants the harassment to stop. You instruct Jane to say nothing about this to David and explain to her that it is important you have a chance to speak with him before he knows of the complaint. You tell her that you will follow up on her complaint as soon as possible and that she is to tell you if anything else occurs before the matter is settled.

The next day, when the night shift custodians arrive, you ask David to step into your office. You begin to explain the complaint that has been made, and David becomes very nervous. After you have spelled out everything that has been alleged, David denies that any of it has happened, except that he has asked Jane out on a date. When he is making his denial, he is visibly nervous. When you ask David what he has said to Jane, he replies that he has only had "normal conversations" with her that occur as he assigns her work. He also says that all the custodians sometimes eat their evening meal together and that they all talk about a variety of subjects. You then tell David that if he has said anything that might be thought of as having sexual connotations, it must stop.

You do not think David has been completely honest with you, and you note that Jane has no apparent reason to file an unfounded complaint. To dig deeper into this matter, you question some other custodians who work with both Jane and David to determine whether they have seen or heard any of these alleged behaviors.

The first custodian you talk with is John, who is new in your building this year. Without being too specific about who has made a complaint or who the alleged perpetrator is, you ask John whether he has noticed anything unusual being said or done that might make others feel uncomfortable. John thinks for a moment and then says that he doesn't think he has heard or seen anything like that. When you ask whether Jane has ever seemed offended by anything anyone has said to her, he answers that she seemed not to like it when David asked her out on a date. John says that David had been polite about it and asked her in front of everyone one evening when they were all eating together. You ask John to please let you know if he notices anything unusual, and he promises you he will. You also ask him not to say anything to anyone else about your conversation.

Immediately you go to find Ingrid, a long-time employee of the district and a very well respected individual. When you pose the same questions to her that you had posed to John, she immediately responds that she has caught David being "nasty" with Jane two times over the past 2 weeks. Both times, he did not know that Ingrid was nearby. When you ask her to tell you specifically what David did or said, she says she saw him looking at Jane "nasty" and that he had said something about seeing her nude.

Your next step is to see whether Ingrid is willing to put in writing what she saw and heard. She responds, "Sure, because no woman needs to be treated that way." You take Ingrid's written statement and then ask her not to say anything to anyone else about what you have discussed with her. Ingrid nods, bids you a good evening, and goes back to her work.

Next, you call David back into your office. He again looks nervous. You tell him you have at least one witness who has confirmed that the things he is alleged to have said and done are true. He tells you that there is no way he can remember everything he has ever said to anyone but that he is sure he has never said anything "ignorant" to Jane. He does say that he sometimes "cusses" but that it is not directed at anyone.

By now, it is time that you leave to supervise a ball game. You remind David not to say anything about this to anyone else. You hope the evening custodial crew makes it through the evening without incident, and you decide to finish your investigation the next day.

When you arrive at school the next day, there is a note on your desk from Jane. She says that she needs to talk to you right away. She leaves her home telephone number and writes that she needs to speak with you before she comes into work today.

Not feeling very good about this whole situation, you decide that you need the advice of your superintendent, Bob Browning. When you tell him about what has been alleged and what you have done with the complaint so far, Mr. Browning immediately asks you who the alleged perpetrator is. When you tell him it is David Jones, the superintendent breathes the words, "Here we go again." Mr. Browning goes on to explain that a similar situation took place several years ago, when David was a custodian at another school in the district. The superintendent agrees to meet with you and David because he is the one who handled the prior incident. He asks you to set up a time when the three of you can meet, preferably this afternoon when David arrives at work. You tell Mr. Browning that you will set up the meeting, and you bid him a good day. Before you hang up, however, you tell him that you have to call Jane because of the message she left the previous evening. He responds that David has probably "done it again."

You immediately contact Jane. She sounds groggy and explains to you that she has had a rather sleepless night because of what she told you about David. She goes on to explain that he apologized to her last night for anything he may have said to offend her. Jane now says that she wants to drop her complaint and asks you whether she can do that.

Scenario #31

SHOT IN THE ARM
(BASIC)

According to school health records, student Steven Clark needs to have a tetanus shot. This was discovered when records were examined during the regular review process. School policy requires that each student have a current tetanus shot in order to attend school in the district.

About 2 weeks ago, the school nurse contacted Steven's mother about this situation, and she first said she would make an appointment to get the shot for her son. Mrs. Clark then called back later that same day to say that she remembered her son having been bitten by a dog about a year ago and that, in the course of treatment for the dog bite, Steven had been given a tetanus shot at the hospital emergency room. Mrs. Clark stated that she would obtain records from the hospital and forward them to the school.

A few days after this telephone conversation, the school nurse had heard nothing more about the shot from Mrs. Clark or from the hospital.

Scenario #32

SHOT IN THE ARM
(ADVANCED)

According to school health records, student Steven Clark needs to have a tetanus shot. This was discovered when records were examined during the regular review process. School policy requires that each student have a current tetanus shot in order to attend school in the district.

About 2 weeks ago, the school nurse contacted Steven's mother about this situation, and she first said she would make an appointment to get the shot for her son. Mrs. Clark then called back later that same day to say that she remembered her son having been bitten by a dog about a year ago and that, in the course of treatment for the dog bite, Steven had been given a tetanus shot at the hospital emergency room. Mrs. Clark stated that she would obtain records from the hospital and forward them to the school.

A few days after this telephone conversation, the school nurse had heard nothing more about the shot from Mrs. Clark or from the hospital.

In a follow-up telephone conversation initiated by the school nurse, Mrs. Clark indicated that she had contacted the hospital and that the hospital was to have sent the records to the school immediately afterward. At this point, the nurse asked whether it would be acceptable for her to call the hospital and request the information. Mrs. Clark indicated that this would be acceptable.

The school nurse immediately called the hospital and discussed the situation with a hospital staff member. The staff person indicated that she would check hospital records and call back to let her know one way or the other. The nurse waited for 3 days to hear back from the hospital, and after hearing nothing, she called the hospital. The same staff person told the nurse that no record could be found of the shot.

During all this time, Steven has continued to attend school. Although district policy requires that a current tetanus shot record be on file before a student can attend school, school nurses routinely waive the requirement for a period of time if the family is working on getting the student a shot or obtaining records.

The nurse called Mrs. Clark this morning (Thursday) and told her that if documentation of the shot was not received by Monday morning, Steven was not to come to school. She informed Mrs. Clark that Steven could return to school as soon as the shot record was received from the hospital or she could document that Steven had received a current tetanus shot.

Mrs. Clark was upset about this because Steven was already struggling in school, and missing school for this "silly" reason would only make things worse. The nurse gave Mrs. Clark your telephone number and extension and called you to inform you of the situation.

Now it's later the same day. You receive a call from Mrs. Clark. Mrs. Clark speaks with you for quite some time, relaying to you all the information the school nurse has already given you. You believe, however, that it is good to listen to Mrs. Clark to let her have her say in the matter. After some time, during a pause in the conversation, you tell Mrs. Clark that you sympathize with her situation but that school district policy mandates that the documentation of her son having received this shot be on record. In fact, you tell her that you could already be in trouble with the district for allowing Steven to attend school even this long without the shot record.

At this point, the conversation takes an unexpected turn. Mrs. Clark suddenly declares to you that this missing shot record does not matter anyhow. You are confused about what she means by this, and you tell her so. She goes on to tell you that a lady she works with had had a similar situation and that the way the lady dealt with it was to sign a religious exemption with the school. This, she says, is all the documentation you will need to let Steven attend school on Monday. She adds that this will also stop the school nurse from harassing her. Mrs. Clark says that she will draw up a notice of exemption based on her religious beliefs and that she will have it signed and notarized. She indicates that her son will deliver it to the school nurse in a sealed envelope first thing Monday morning.

Scenario #33

TROUBLE HAS ARRIVED, OR HAS TROUBLE ARRIVED?

Bobby Blankenship enrolled in your school on October 17 of the current school year, transferring in from a school in an adjoining state. He is 17 and a sophomore.

After 3 days of attendance, you begin to hear rumors that Bobby is bragging to others about his illegal exploits in his former school and in his former neighborhood. You also get word, through your "principal's grapevine," that Bobby is threatening other students, saying that he will beat them up if they do not give him money. You can find no students who will say that Bobby has threatened them.

This situation concerns you. You go to the main file on this student to gather any information available about Bobby from files that have been transferred from his former school. When you look at Bobby's transcript, you find that he received average grades 2 years ago but received poor grades last year in his former school district's alternative high school.

You continue your investigation regarding this student by talking with the person who registered him, Terry Greer. Terry is the school's academic counselor. Terry recalls that the student's father mentioned the boy had been in trouble at his former school and that his mother had agreed to let Bobby live with his father in an effort to get him back on the right track.

You finally call Bobby into your office to speak with him. When you question Bobby about what is going on, he speaks to you in a very respectful manner. Bobby tells you that he was in trouble at his old school but that he is trying to put his past behind him and get a fresh start. He denies that he has been talking to others about his former illegal exploits and also denies threatening others.

Bobby does add, however, that even if he were talking about what he had done "back home," it was not against school rules.

As the person in the school who is ultimately responsible for students' well-being and safety, you are still concerned about Bobby and what negative influence he might have on others, although you at least partially believe that he is sincere in trying to start over.

Scenario #34

FIRE DRILL CAPER

Today you conduct one of your regularly scheduled fire drills. Everyone is evacuating the building nicely, classes are assembling outside, and teachers are taking roll. About 1 minute after everyone has evacuated the building, you get word that two female students are missing from Mrs. Smith's class. You immediately go to where Mrs. Smith's class is assembled.

You ask whether Mrs. Smith is sure the girls were in the class when they all evacuated. She indicates that she is positive the girls were in class before the class left the room. In fact, she remembers that she had to ask one of the girls to get into her seat after the tardy bell had rung.

About this time, the fire chief walks over to you. It seems that he happened to be driving by when he saw all the students evacuating the building. He assumed that this was just a drill but wanted to stop just to make sure and to see whether he could do anything to help.

Scenario #35
CHECK IT OUT

Rebekah Gregg, the school librarian, comes to your office to speak with you about finances and the needs of the school library. You invite her in, ask your secretary to hold all your calls, and begin to speak with Ms. Gregg about the situation.

As Ms. Gregg enters, you notice that she has some papers in her hand. As she begins to talk to you, you realize that the papers detail all the school library's needs that are necessary for the library to meet state standards. She indicates that the former principal had neglected the library financially over the past few years and that the library was now well below state standards in terms of number of current volumes available in certain areas. She also explains that she has devised a plan to alleviate the library's problems. She says that the plan will need to be implemented over the next 4 years and that it will involve a financial commitment from the school budget.

As you continue to listen to Ms. Gregg, you learn things about library standards you never knew before. You sympathize with Ms. Gregg and tell her that you understand the library needs some attention; finally, you ask her how much this plan will cost. You are shocked when Ms. Gregg tells you the amount. You do some quick calculations in your head and estimate that it would take roughly one third of your building's allocated budget over each of the next 4 years to do what the librarian is proposing.

After a pause to let the impact of this proposal sink in, Ms. Gregg asks you about the feasibility of the implementation of this plan. At the same time, she also reminds you that accreditation will be taking place 2 years from now and that one area scrutinized closely is the library.

Scenario #36

WHAT'S GOOD FOR THE GOOSE

Johnny Seir is a student in your school who has an Individualized Education Plan (IEP). Johnny's disability relates to behavior. Johnny has already been suspended from school for 7 days this year. No changes have been made this year to his IEP.

Today, 3 days before winter break, Johnny was involved in a fight in the school with another student. The other student, Sam Stevens, has average grades and has never received a discipline notice at your school. He is also a starting guard on the sophomore basketball team.

From what you can piece together by listening to both boys' stories, Johnny had been making crude remarks to and about Sam for weeks. Many of the comments had been sexual in nature and also involved Sam's sister and mother. Sam had asked Johnny to leave him alone on several occasions, but Johnny simply would not stop. Sam and Johnny have math, physical education, and lunch together. Sam has told no one in authority at school what has been happening.

Today, things came to a head at lunch when Johnny again made comments to Sam about him and his family and then pushed him. Sam did not try to walk away, but he did not retaliate either. Johnny pushed Sam again, this time knocking him into a table and spilling another student's drink, which got on Sam's jacket sleeve. This time, Sam pushed back, knocking Johnny into another table. Johnny's hand landed in another student's mashed potatoes and gravy, which he then slung onto Sam. A full-fledged fight then broke out, with each boy hitting the other several times. Johnny ended up with a black eye, and Sam ended up with a bloody nose.

This situation would usually result in a minimum of 5 days' out-of-school suspension for each student, based on the severity of the fight. If suspended even the minimum number of days, Sam will not be able to participate in the conference junior varsity holiday basketball tournament.

You are now faced with how to discipline each student.

Scenario #37
FIZZLE

The local salesman for Rio Cola, a national brand-name soft drink, calls to ask whether you are happy with your current soft drink vendor. Currently, another national brand is sold in your school's vending machines and concession stands. You reply that you are happy but also tell the salesman that your contract with that vendor will expire at the end of this school year.

The salesman tells you that if you agree to selling Rio brand soft drinks in your school's vending machines and concession stands for the next 3 years, his company will contribute many things to your school. He says the contributions would include cash up front, a new scoreboard for the gym, academic incentives for the students, and appreciation items for the teachers. When you ask how much all of this could amount to in terms of dollars, his one-word answer is "substantial."

You have a good relationship with the salesman representing the soft drink brand that is sold in your school now. His company has contributed to sponsoring sports events and has paid for an expensive motivational speaker to come to your school for an assembly each of the past 5 years. The teachers have also enjoyed the end-of-the-year appreciation banquet this company has sponsored.

The salesman from Rio Cola wants to know what he would have to do to get your business.

Scenario #38
FOR YOUR REFERENCE

James Wade is a custodian at your school. For the past 3 mornings, James has called in sick, saying that he has the flu and is too sick to get out of bed, much less come to work. Because this procedure is within district sick-leave policy and James has not used all his sick days for the year yet, you wish him a speedy recovery and hang up the telephone.

Later in the afternoon of James's third sick day, you receive a call from a Mr. Larry Conoyer. Mr. Conoyer owns LC Maintenance Company in a nearby town. He indicates that James has listed you as a reference on his application for a position as maintenance supervisor with LC Maintenance and that he is calling to ask you about James's work habits, attendance, and so on. You were not aware that James was seeking other employment, but you can't fault a man for trying to better his position in life, so you agree to speak with Mr. Conoyer.

You tell Mr. Conoyer that James generally does very fine work when he comes to work. This leads him to ask about James's general attendance record. You tell him that James occasionally misses work but only when he is so sick that he has to stay in bed, like today. This comment is followed by a long pause on Mr. Conoyer's part, after which he tells you that he interviewed James Wade at his office this morning at about 9:30. Mr. Conoyer then thanks you for your time, tells you that this is all the information he will need, and then hangs up.

Scenario #39

GONE TO THE DOGS

This morning, you receive a call from Detective Jim Ortiz of the county sheriff's department. You know Detective Ortiz from several community projects you have worked on together. The detective exchanges greetings with you and then gets to the point of his call.

Detective Ortiz asks you whether you are aware that there is a drug problem at your school. You answer that you are sure some students who attend your school experiment with drugs but that you are not aware of any major drug users or sellers. You certainly are not aware of any using or selling going on at school.

The detective then informs you he has received information from a very reliable source that a group of six boys in your school are not only heavy drug users but frequently sell drugs at school. In fact, those who "do" drugs in the county know they can always get drugs from these six boys, either at school or outside school. When you ask the detective who these boys are, he says that he doesn't know but that his source told him it is students you would least expect.

This information alarms you, but you are not sure what immediate action to take, especially because you do not know who the alleged drug dealers and users are. Detective Ortiz suggests that his department's two drug dogs, along with their trainers, who are also police officers, be stationed at the exit doors one day next week as the students leave for the day. He says that because your building only has these two ways for students to exit, he is sure to identify the perpetrators.

The detective indicates that he can have plenty of other officers on hand to make arrests if necessary. He thinks this "show of force" on school property would deter these boys from dealing drugs at school, even if they are not caught, and would also deter others who might have similar aspirations. For obvious reasons, Detective Ortiz suggests that this operation not be announced to anyone beforehand.

Scenario #40

LIVING IN SHANGRI-LA

Paul Croteau is a very bright 17-year-old student in your school, but he gets poor grades, is constantly tardy to his classes, is sometimes truant from individual classes, and is often truant from school. During the first 2 months of school, you see Paul in your office on the average of three times per week. You have tried every sort of discipline available to you, including a conference with him and his father and a suspension. Nothing has seemed to have had any impact on Paul with regard to these problems.

In the first week of November, Paul is again truant from school, and you call his father at work to let him know that Paul will be disciplined for his behavior. Mr. Croteau is very cooperative with you, but he does not know how to help improve his son's attendance habits.

During your conversation with Mr. Croteau, you learn that he brings Paul to school every day, or else Paul gets a ride with his girlfriend, who is also a student at your school. Mr. Croteau indicates that, on many occasions when Paul has been truant, he has left for school with his girlfriend. He does not know why Paul has not arrived at school on these days.

When you suggest that Paul ride the bus every day to help ensure that he arrives at school, Mr. Croteau seems reluctant to accept this solution and, in fact, says before the conversation ends that this just will not work. You wonder why, but do not think much of it at the time.

Later, as you think more about this situation, you wonder whether the reason why Mr. Croteau does not readily accept the idea of Paul riding the bus is that a bus for your school doesn't come by his house because he does not live in the district. You surmise that Paul is only coming to this school to be with his girlfriend.

As a first step in following up on your hunch, you send a letter to Mr. Croteau in which you discuss your most recent conversation with him, tell him of future disciplinary action, and thank him for his time in speaking with you. You send it to the address on Paul's records, which indicates that he is a student in your district. Your reasoning is that if the Croteaus have not lived at this address for any length of time, the post office will return the letter to you.

Sure enough, the letter is returned by the post office in about 2 weeks. Stamped on the envelope is ADDRESSEE UNKNOWN.

Scenario #41
UNWELCOME VISITOR

You are walking down the hallway one day late in September at a time when all students should be in class. You see a rather young man you do not recognize. You don't think too much of it because there are valid reasons why someone you do not know might be in the school. The young man looks to be about 20 years of age and is dressed in nice jeans, a designer sweatshirt, and new sneakers.

As is your custom when you encounter someone in the school whom you do not know, you ask the young man if you can help him. He replies, "No, man," and keeps walking. You are taken aback by his response, but as he takes his second step away from you, you ask him whether he has checked in at the office. He replies, "No, man," again, but before he has the chance to walk away again, you ask him to please come with you.

He does follow you to the office, where you ask him to sign in at the guest register. After he has done so, you ask him what business he has at the school. He replies that he is a former student and that he is here to see one of his favorite former teachers, Ms. Druid. You explain to this young man that teachers cannot be visited during school hours because of the disruption it causes in the school.

At this, the man becomes very upset and says that the former principal let him visit any teacher anytime he wanted to. You explain again in a calm but firm voice that visitors are not welcome in teachers' classrooms during the school day. At this, the young man replies, "This is bull_ _ _ _," and walks out of your office. You follow him, assuming that he is leaving the building, but he immediately takes a turn toward Ms. Druid's classroom instead.

Scenario #42

THE ACCIDENT

Near the end of school one day, you receive a call from the school nurse, Gina Grover. She asks you to come to her office. She says that it is "sort of" an emergency but that no one is in physical danger. She says she would rather explain herself in person.

You go to the nurse's office immediately, and as soon as you walk in you smell a foul odor. When you ask what the smell is, Mrs. Grover indicates that this is what she wants to talk with you about.

The nurse then begins to explain to you that Eric Jeling was sent to her by one of his teachers because he had had an accident in his pants. You readily recognize the student's name because you have seen him in your office on several occasions for disciplinary matters. You ask whether the student has any health problems that would cause this, and the nurse says that he has no health problems she is aware of. Mrs. Grover goes on to say that Eric says his teacher would not give him a pass to go to the rest room when Eric told him that he "really had to go." You ask Mrs. Grover whether she has called Eric's parents yet, and she says she has not.

When you ask Mrs. Grover whether everything is under control, she says that Eric is cleaning up, that she has found some clean clothes for him, and that everything seems to be under control for the time being.

You leave the nurse's office and, after checking Eric's schedule, go to talk with Mr. Stevens, the teacher whose class Eric was in when the accident happened. You arrive at Mr. Stevens's class and ask the teacher to step outside for a moment to speak with you. He gives his students some quick instructions and then steps into the hallway where both you and he can talk privately yet still see his students.

Mr. Stevens listens as you tell him what you know about this situation, according to the story Eric told the nurse. Mr. Stevens responds that this story is essentially just what happened. He goes on to tell you that his class policy is that students only receive two passes per semester, to be used for whatever reason (e.g., rest room, nurse, counselor, locker). He says that after a student's two passes are used, the student does not have permission to leave the room for any reason, save a major emergency like a fire.

Eric, you find out, had used both of his passes to go to the rest room during the first 3 weeks of school. Therefore, when he asked to go to the rest room today, Mr. Stevens told Eric that he did not have any more passes to use and, furthermore, that if Eric had walked out of class to use the rest room, Mr. Stevens would have marked him as truant from his class and written up a disciplinary referral to the principal.

Scenario #43
HAPPY HOLIDAYS

On December 17, one of your staff asks to speak with you. As is your custom, you reply, "Sure," and invite the teacher in. He sits down and begins to explain to you that he has a concern. He says that the many decorated trees, lights, and other decorations around the school that, in his estimation, celebrate Christmas, offend him. He goes on to explain that he does not come from a Christian heritage and that he does not believe he should have to work around such images.

In your conversation with him, you ask whether he has seen any truly religious symbols displayed, such as nativity scenes. He responds that he has not seen any nativity scenes or other truly religious symbols but that everyone knows that decorated trees, lights, red stockings, bells, and wreaths symbolize the Christian holiday of Christmas.

This teacher asks that you demand all decorations be taken down because of the separation of church and state issues involved in these items being displayed in a public school.

Scenario #44

WHAT DO I DO NOW?
(BASIC)

Andrew Cherio is a student in your school whom you know very well; he has been referred to your office for discipline before from a variety of teachers. Mrs. Weems has sent him to your office an average of twice a week for the past 3 weeks. Mrs. Weems, a science teacher, has sent Andrew to the office for disruptive and disrespectful behavior, and he is the only student she has referred to you in the past 3 years.

You have used a variety of disciplinary approaches with Andrew. You have had conferences with his parents (both over the telephone and in person), given him after-school and Saturday detentions, placed him in in-school suspension, and suspended him out of school.

About a week ago, you drew up a behavior contract that Andrew, his parents, and you signed. The contract stipulated both negative and positive consequences for Andrew's behavior. Neither this nor anything else you have tried seems to have had much of a positive impact on Andrew's behavior.

Today, Mrs. Weems again sends Andrew to your office. Along with the discipline referral, she also sends a sealed envelope. In the envelope, you find a note from Mrs. Weems in which she pleads that you either do something that will change Andrew's behavior in her class or remove Andrew from the class. The discipline referral says that Andrew was talking to his neighbor nonstop while Mrs. Weems was giving very important directions for a potentially dangerous lab activity and that he would not stop after repeated warnings.

Scenario #45

WHAT DO I DO NOW?
(ADVANCED)

Andrew Cherio is a student in your school whom you know very well; he has been referred to your office for discipline before from a variety of teachers. Mrs. Weems has sent him to your office an average of twice a week for the past 3 weeks. Mrs. Weems, a science teacher, has sent Andrew to the office for disruptive and disrespectful behavior, and he is the only student she has referred to you in the past 3 years.

You have used a variety of disciplinary approaches with Andrew. You have had conferences with his parents (both over the telephone and in person), given him after-school and Saturday detentions, placed him in-school suspension, and suspended him out of school.

About a week ago, you drew up a behavior contract that Andrew, his parents, and you signed. The contract stipulated both negative and positive consequences for Andrew's behavior. Neither this nor anything else you have tried seems to have had much of a positive impact on Andrew's behavior.

Today, Mrs. Weems again sends Andrew to your office. Along with the discipline referral, she also sends a sealed envelope. In the envelope you find a note from Mrs. Weems in which she pleads that you either do something that will change Andrew's behavior in her class or remove Andrew from the class. The discipline referral says that Andrew was talking to his neighbor nonstop while Mrs. Weems was giving very important directions for a potentially dangerous lab activity and that he would not stop after repeated warnings.

You ask Andrew to sit in a chair in your office, and he does so. You question him about his antics in Mrs. Weems's class, and he claims that this time he really did not do anything. He says that Frank Blume was doing the talking and that she thought it was Andrew.

Desiring to give Andrew the benefit of the doubt, you walk to Mrs. Weems's room to speak with her about the situation. When you tell her what Andrew said, she says it was definitely Andrew who was talking because she even saw his lips moving. She seems perturbed that you investigated what the student had told you even though she had documented the situation on the discipline referral.

You return to your office to confront Andrew. Andrew again maintains his innocence, but you must believe what the teacher has said, and you tell Andrew so. In your talk with Andrew, you also indicate that his disturbing Mrs. Weems's class is well within the realm of possibility, as it has happened many times. Andrew cannot argue this fact.

You decide that it is time to take more drastic action. Even though this is a class disruption situation for which a student usually is disciplined with detentions, Andrew has been sent to you many times this year for the same sort of conduct. You decide to suspend him from school for 5 days, and you warn him that he will have to go to a hearing before the superintendent and the school board the next time he is referred to your office. Andrew is upset and still claims his innocence. He also seems disturbed that he may have to go before the superintendent and school board if his behavior does not change soon.

When you call Andrew's parents to let them know of Andrew's discipline, they react about as usual. Although they do not like the idea of suspension, they agree that it is time that Andrew suffer more severe consequences. They are growing weary of hearing from you and others at the school, and they hope that this action may "do the trick." With this, you write up all the necessary documents, including forwarding information to Andrew's teachers that he will be suspended for the next 5 days.

After school, two of Andrew's teachers come to you and say, "Thank you." Not thinking of Andrew at the time, you do not know what they are thanking you for. They explain that a day without Andrew in the classroom is almost like a day of vacation, and they are thankful that they will not have to deal with him for a week. They both comment that Andrew is a likeable boy but that he can bring a lesson to ruin by his constant disruptions. You end the conversation by saying, "You're welcome."

All is well when you leave school for the evening, but you receive a call the first thing the next morning from Andrew's father. Mr. Cherio is not quite his usual cooperative self this morning. He is upset because Andrew says that he absolutely did not talk the last time Mrs. Weems asked him not to. He says that she has a right to keep a close watch on the boy because of his prior behavior but that she does not have the right to make up things just to get a "troublemaker" out of her classroom. Mr. Cherio says that Andrew has many faults but that lying is not one of them, and he demands that the suspension be dropped. He agrees that Andrew could receive some discipline for disrupting Mrs. Weems's class in the first place and having to be warned but that he simply will not allow Andrew to be suspended. Mr. Cherio also tells you that this is his day off and that he would very much like to come to school to meet with you and Mrs. Weems.

DISCUSSION
STARTER QUESTIONS

Discussion Starter Questions are provided here in an effort to share some of the personal practical knowledge of the author with the users of this book. You may wonder why the questions are located in a separate chapter, as opposed to at the end of each Mail Basket Item and Scenario. The reason for this is flexibility. With some uses of the book, it might be desirable for respondents to develop their own questions to ask. In other uses, respondents might be given the benefit of these starter questions.

Thinking of one's own questions to be asked in developing solutions to situations that administrators encounter is one major purpose of this work. Although there is some benefit in learning how to find the answers to questions, the true skill and expertise is in knowing what information will be needed to come to a conclusion about how to solve a problem.

Mail Basket Items

Mail Basket #1 – Letter From a Concerned School Neighbor

1. In responding to this complaint, should your purpose be to stop any students from cutting across this man's property, or should it be to catch those students who are already guilty of doing this?

2. Should you call Mr. Kyle to let him know what you are doing about this problem? Explain.
3. How will you keep students from cutting across Mr. Kyle's property?
4. If students are warned yet continue to cut across Mr. Kyle's property, what action should be taken next?
5. If you decide to contact parents about this situation, what sort of communication will you use?

Mail Basket #2 – Hand-Written Note Complaining of Son's Mistreatment

1. What information should you gather to be able to respond appropriately to this letter? How will you gather this information?
2. Is it appropriate to tell Mr. Smith what discipline, if any, the boy who threatened his son will receive?
3. Should you call the superintendent to let him know about this situation because Mr. Smith says he may call the superintendent?

Mail Basket #3 – Telephone Message From Sheriff's Department

1. Is it appropriate for a police officer to question a student at school regarding an incident that happened outside school?
2. If you allow the student to be questioned, under what circumstances should parents first be informed? Are there any circumstances under which parents should not be informed of the questioning?
3. Does the student's age have any bearing on whether you will allow questioning? Explain.
4. If the student is a minor, do juvenile authorities need to be involved? Explain.

Mail Basket #4 – Budget Memo From Department Chairperson

1. Was your request made far enough in advance?
2. Does Karen Honet understand the basics of the budgeting process and how her information ties into the entire budget? Explain.
3. How will you approach getting the information that you need in a timely manner?
4. How will you address this issue with Karen Honet so that it does not happen again?
5. Will the Science Department be penalized in any way as a result of lack of information about budget needs (be given the same budget as last year even though other departments are receiving an increase)?
6. If past administrators have shown a pattern of unmet timelines regarding the budget, how should this be addressed?

Mail Basket #5 – Request for Band Field Trip

1. Is it appropriate to take 40 band students out of school for a day to "entertain" elementary school students? Explain.
2. Is this activity essential to the band program? Explain.

3. Does this activity build public relations for your school? If so, does that make it appropriate? Explain.
4. Does the fact that this activity has taken place for the past 10 years have any bearing on your decision? Explain.
5. Would it matter on what day/date the field trip was scheduled? Explain.
6. Has Mrs. McLafferty followed proper procedures in requesting this field trip?

Mail Basket #6 – Letter Regarding Assembly Program

1. Would it be reasonable for Ms. Druid to have the authority to book this program without consulting you? Would past carte blanche by former administrators to make such decisions have any bearing on how you handled this situation?
2. Could it ever be appropriate to have an assembly that is presented from a Christian perspective and during which biblical references are used? Explain. Does this depend on the community in which the school is located?
3. If you decide that the assembly is inappropriate, because the $100 deposit is not refundable, will you reimburse Ms. Druid the $100 out of school funds? If so, from which fund would this reimbursement be taken? Would precedents set by former administrators affect your decision in any way?
4. Is there an appropriate dollar limit that should be paid for presenters of school assembly programs? Explain.

Mail Basket #7 – Memo Regarding Professional Development Activity

1. Is assessing professional development needs an important activity? Explain. If a needs assessment is not used, how should professional development activities be determined?
2. Would it be important for you to know more about how the needs assessment will take place? Explain.
3. Is it a good practice to require after-school meetings when after-school activities are taking place that require faculty sponsors/coaches? If not, how will you solve the problem of an acceptable time for the faculty meeting?
4. If the faculty meeting takes place on November 18, how will students be supervised while waiting for sponsors/coaches to be finished with the meeting?

Mail Basket #8 – Note Regarding No Heat in Room

1. To whom would you speak first about this situation—Jon Stevens or maintenance personnel? Explain.
2. What information will you have to gather to solve this problem?
3. Which issue is of most concern in this situation—Jon Stevens's health, student learning, or lack of follow-up by maintenance personnel? Explain.

Mail Basket #9 – Discipline Notice: Cheating

1. Is this a situation that should come to your office as a discipline referral? Explain.

2. Assume that you think this is a situation you should handle. What disciplinary action will you take? When you take this disciplinary action, do you need to known any other facts before making your decision? Explain. Will you speak with the teacher before taking disciplinary action? Why or why not?

3. Assume that you think this is a situation the teacher should have handled. How will you approach the teacher? What suggestions would you make to the teacher in handling this situation?

Mail Basket #10 – Telephone Message From Parent Regarding Suspension

1. Assume that suspension for truancy is a policy in your school/district. How will you explain the disciplinary benefits of this to Mr. Skipavovich?

2. Assume that your school's/district's policy is that zeroes are given for all work missed during the period of a suspension. Should you ever make an exception to this policy? Explain.

3. Should John's suspension be repealed and replaced with some other form of discipline on the basis of arguments presented in Mr. Skipavovich's telephone message?

4. What information will you need to gather before returning Mr. Skipavovich's telephone call?

5. Mr. Skipavovich's telephone message was received at 9:17 a.m. By what time, if any, do you think this message should be returned? Explain.

6. Should your immediate supervisor be informed about this parent's complaint? If yes, before or after you return the telephone call?

Mail Basket #11 – Note Regarding Janitors' Smoking

1. To whom will you want to speak first in regard to this note? Explain.

2. Mr. Matson has asked that you not tell the custodial staff he gave you this information. Assume that your investigation confirms his suspicions. How can you address the situation and respect Mr. Matson's wishes?

3. Assume that it is difficult in your school/district to provide dedicated, loyal, and efficient custodial staff but that your current staff has all these qualities. Will this change how you handle the issue? Is it ever acceptable to ignore such violation of rules? Explain.

Mail Basket #12 – Note From Counselor Regarding Student With ADD

1. Should you verify that Bradley has attention deficit disorder (ADD)? If so, how will you do this?

2. Do any laws protect students with ADD? If so, discuss these.

3. Assume that Mrs. Wilson's concerns are valid. Will you allow Bradley to bring the tape recorder to class? Do any privacy issues need to be considered before you make your decision? Should the teachers be involved in this decision?

4. Whether or not you allow Bradley to use a tape recorder in class, are there any issues that teachers need to be made aware of? Explain.

5. What information will need to be gathered before Mrs. Wilson's call is returned?
6. Who should return Mrs. Wilson's call? Explain.

Mail Basket #13 – Telephone Message From Law Firm

1. Is it appropriate for a school/district to receive contributions from businesses in the community? Explain.
2. Steve Johnson would like to have a mailing list, presumably for students, parents, or some other group. Is it appropriate to distribute this information to a business concern?
3. Should you take the contribution? If so, what should the stipulations be? If not, how will you explain your decision to Mr. Johnson without offending him?

Mail Basket #14 – Discipline Notice: Fighting and Profanity

1. What should be done first in responding to this situation?
2. After physical injuries have been addressed, what information will you need to gather before you respond to this situation? With whom will you want to speak? Does any of your information need to be in writing? Explain.
3. Is this a situation in which law enforcement officials need to be involved? Explain.
4. If both girls threw punches in this situation, does it matter from a disciplinary or legal standpoint who threw the first punch? Explain.
5. Assume that Jean only used profanity but did not fight back when Joan punched her. Should she be disciplined? Explain. If her nose is broken, will this have any bearing on your decision?

Mail Basket #15 – Telephone Message From Superintendent

1. Will you need to gather any information before you return the superintendent's call?
2. How will you respond if the superintendent does not agree with your disciplinary decision and wants you to count the day of suspension as an excused absence instead? Can you override the superintendent's decision? Explain.

Mail Basket #16 – Discipline Notice: Student Asking "Dumb" Questions

1. Is this a situation that should come to your office as a discipline referral? Explain.
2. Assume that you think this is a situation you should handle. What disciplinary action will you take? Do you need to know any other facts before making your decision? Will you speak with the teacher before taking disciplinary action? Why or why not?
3. Assume that you think this is a situation the teacher should have handled. How will you approach the teacher? What suggestions would you make to the teacher in handling this situation?

4. Is the teacher's use of the word *dumb* to describe a student's behavior appropriate? If so, why? If not, how could the discipline notice be written better? Should the discipline notice be rewritten before you take action on it?

Mail Basket #17 – Teacher Received Letter Regarding Excessive Homework

1. The teacher has asked you what she should do. What will your response be? Will you want to get any information from the teacher before you formulate a response? If so, what information will you need?
2. Should you call the parent, Ms. Donna Smith, before she has a chance to call the teacher? Explain.
3. Should you or the teacher speak with Dave about this situation? If so, should you do so before or after speaking with his mother?
4. Assume that you, along with the teacher, determine the amount of homework she is giving is appropriate for the subject and grade level. Should you make any special accommodations for Dave in this particular instance, or in general?

Mail Basket #18 – Note From Teacher Regarding Field Trips

1. Who should be responsible for developing the policy on students taking field trips?
2. Should teachers have any input on whether a student attends a field trip with another class? Explain.
3. Should the student who cannot make up labs after school have been allowed to attend the field trip? Why or why not?
4. Who should decide whether a particular field trip is appropriate for students' needs?
5. Should factors other than academics be considered when deciding whether a field trip is appropriate? For example, would a field trip to attend a cultural event be appropriate?

Mail Basket #19 – Request for Favor From School Board Member

1. Is it ethical for a school board member to approach you in this way? Explain.
2. What will your response to Jan Kominski be?
3. Should you contact anyone else about Ms. Kominski's request? Explain.

Mail Basket #20 – Telephone Message About a Teacher's Comments

1. Should you take appointments on a short notice if you can fit such an appointment into your schedule? Explain.
2. If your current schedule will not allow you to see this parent, should you make cancellations in order to see her? Explain.
3. If you cannot see the parent right away, what should you do?
4. In this case, is there any information you can gather before you return Mrs. Stephenson's call that might help you in your response to her?

5. What information should you ask Mrs. Stephenson for when you speak with her?

6. Is it necessary that you meet in person to solve this issue? Would you need more information to determine this? If so, what information would you need?

Mail Basket #21 – Note From Teacher Regarding In-School Suspension

1. What will your first course of action be in responding to this complaint? What fact finding will you need to do? From whom will you need to gather information?

2. Is it acceptable for a teacher to refuse to do something even though some problems may need to be resolved regarding the issue?

3. Is this a problem that should be addressed by you, the principal? Explain.

Mail Basket #22 – Parent Complaint Regarding Birth Film Shown In Class

1. Is a parent's signature on a registration form adequate permission to show this video in class? Explain.

2. Is it appropriate for this video to be shown in class regardless of whether special permission was obtained from parents? Explain. Who should decide what materials are appropriate for this class?

3. How will you respond to the upset parent, now that the video has already been shown and her son has already been exposed to what she considers unacceptable material?

4. What, if anything, can you do to prevent complaints such as this in the future?

Mail Basket #23 – Note From Secretary Regarding Student Athletes Arrested

1. Was it both proper and legal for the sheriff's deputy to share this information with you? Explain.

2. Should you take any disciplinary action, considering this situation happened outside of school? Should any action, such as temporary suspension from the team or removal from the team, be taken in the light of this information? Does whether or not the boys will be prosecuted have any bearing on your decision?

3. Do you need more information to make any of your decisions? If so, how will you go about obtaining this information if Deputy Mary Shew cannot be reached today?

4. If any action is taken, should your decision be make today? Does the importance of tonight's game have any bearing on your decision?

5. Did your secretary take proper action in trying to give this information to Coach Jenkins? Why or why not?

6. Would a call to the students' parents be appropriate whether or not any other action is taken? Explain.

Mail Basket #24 – Student's Note

1. What in this note might be of concern to you?

2. Should you attempt to identify who "Jessica" and "John" are, considering their last names are not listed on this note? If so, how will you go about it?

3. Assume that you can identify the author of this note and the obvious boyfriend. Should any action be taken? Should you call the students' parents? Explain.

Mail Basket #25 – Letter From Parent of Student With IEP

1. What information do you need in order to respond to this parent? Will you need to get some of this information from Mrs. Lee? Explain.

2. Will you allow this parent to sit in on some of her daughter's classes? Why or why not?

3. Are any legal issues involved here? Explain.

4. Do you agree with the parent's assessment of the student's actions that she is getting into trouble for doing "silly" things? Explain. How will you address this issue with the parent?

5. How will you determine whether Mrs. Lee needs to change the way she is responding to this student?

Scenarios

Scenario #1 – It's a Hit!

1. Of all the issues involved in this situation, what should be your highest priority?

2. Should law enforcement authorities be contacted in this situation? Explain.

3. Assuming that you have the information to do so, should you contact the car driver's school? Would it make a difference if that school were in your district? Should the driver be disciplined at his school, considering the accident happened at a school bus stop?

4. Should Tamika's parents be contacted? If so, at what point in your dealing with this issue should they be contacted?

Scenario #2 – Words Will Ever Hurt Me

1. Should you (or can you) require that Gina and the offending girls participate in mediation? Explain.

2. Should the offending girls be questioned despite Gina's and her mother's request? Explain.

3. If a fight over this situation were to occur, would the fact that Gina has told you about this situation in advance change how you would handle her discipline for participating in a fight? Explain.

4. Because Gina is being threatened with physical harm, should law enforcement officials be involved? Explain.

5. Assume that you grant Gina's and her mother's request and do not talk to the offending girls. Are there any precautionary measures you can take to help ensure that this situation does not result in physical violence? Explain.

Scenario #3 – Fan-atical (Basic)

1. What is the best way to approach this parent? What will you say to the parent when you approach him in the stands? Would this depend on whether, in your estimation, the officiating had in fact been poor? Explain.

2. Could anything have been done beforehand (by you, the coach, or anyone else) to help keep this type of situation from happening? Explain.

3. Will this incident change the way you supervise at activities? Explain.

4. Should any follow-up be initiated in regard to this situation? Explain.

Scenario #4 – Fan-atical (Advanced)

1. Should you have done anything differently in your response up to this point? Explain.

2. What will your immediate response to Mr. Roelker be? What will your long-term response be? Does he need to be banned from attending games, or can you legally and morally do this? Explain.

3. Considering what happened at the previous basketball game, do you need to say anything to Mrs. Roelker at this point? Should you have talked with her already?

4. Can you do anything teamwide or schoolwide to prevent this type of situation from occurring at basketball games or at other sports? Explain.

5. Could you have done anything differently at this game that would have helped prevent this situation from occurring? Explain.

6. What are the implications of Mr. Roelker's actions for the entire school and its activity/athletic programs?

7. Should your immediate supervisor be informed about this situation? Explain.

Scenario #5 – Room for a Change

1. In considering this situation, should you require written documentation of Jim's medical problem? Would that help you in the decision-making process? If you ask for documentation, are you insulting Jim? Explain.

2. Should you consider any other possible solutions to the problem?

3. Are there any legal ramifications if you do not grant Jim his request? Explain.

4. Should your immediate supervisor be informed about this situation? Explain.

Scenario #6 – Hair Today, Gone Tomorrow

1. Is it acceptable for school employees to leave the building during break time to take care of personal business? Explain.
2. Do you have enough documentation at this time to take disciplinary action toward Tom Stiles? Explain.
3. Should this incident be documented in Tom's file? Explain.
4. Would you change anything about how this situation has been handled up to this point? Explain.
5. Should you agree to meet with Tom and his lawyer? If you do agree to meet, should you also have some representation?
6. Should your immediate supervisor be informed about this situation? Explain.

Scenario #7 – Fix the Problem (Basic)

1. Did you prepare properly for this meeting? Should you have had all of Michael's teachers at this meeting?
2. How will you investigate whether Ms. Theim's accusations are true?
3. If you discover that accommodations delineated in Michael's IEP have not been made by the teachers, should the grades be adjusted? Explain.
4. If accommodations have not been made, will this change any of your policies and procedures regarding students with IEPs? Explain.
5. If you discover that teachers have been making all the accommodations outlined in Michael's IEP, how will you document this? How will you answer Ms. Theim's complaint?

Scenario #8 – Fix the Problem (Advanced)

1. Did you prepare properly for the original meeting? Should you have had all of Michael's teachers at this meeting?
2. Did you learn anything about the preparation of IEPs from this situation? Explain.
3. Even though the IEP did not specify exactly how long Michael was to be given to make up assignments, do you think you have enough evidence to verify that the school has met its obligations regarding the IEP? Why or why not?
4. How will you prepare for the meeting to take place 2 days from now?
5. Do you need anyone else's help in deciding how you will handle this situation? Explain.
6. Should your immediate supervisor or the superintendent be contacted about this situation? Explain.

Scenario #9 – I Have a Great Job!

1. Could the teacher have handled this situation better, from the inception of the idea to her response to Ryan?
2. Should Ryan's father be allowed to speak to the class? Why or why not?

3. Should Ryan's absence from school today be considered excused? Would you need more information to decide this?
4. What steps could you take to prevent such a situation from happening in the future?
5. Does your immediate supervisor need to be informed of this situation? Explain.

Scenario #10 – You Make the Call

1. Was it acceptable for Coach Jenkins to use the word *retarded* in any way in responding to the boys' towel flipping? If it is unacceptable, what will you say to Coach Jenkins?
2. Is it ever appropriate to tell a parent what disciplinary action is taken toward an employee? Explain.
3. Should Kamal have been disciplined differently for his behavior when it occurred? Should Kamal be disciplined now?
4. On the basis of what Coach Jenkins has told you about this situation, do you have any general concerns about supervision in the locker room or gym?
5. Should the superintendent be informed of this situation and your response to it, as Mrs. Haddad suggests? Explain.

Scenario #11 – Balancing Act

1. Is Mrs. Suarez's request reasonable? Is it always possible to schedule classes so that teachers have approximately the same class loads? Explain.
2. Will you attempt to investigate why the class sizes are different? Will you try to adjust class sizes? Will Mrs. Suarez's threat to file a grievance have any bearing on your decision? Explain.
3. Will this complaint change the way the master schedule is created in the future? Explain.

Scenario #12 – Too Hot to Handle

1. Has this situation been handled correctly up to this point? Should the student have been taken off the bus? Explain.
2. What could have been done if the parent could not have picked up the student immediately?
3. Should the student have been left alone in the office to speak with his mother? Explain.
4. How will you respond to the parent's complaint? Do you need more information before you can give your response?

Scenario #13 – Drug Store (Basic)

1. Do you have enough information to question and/or search Stacey and Lisa? If so, should you just question, or also search? Does your answer depend on any other factors, such as prior disciplinary history of the students?
2. Assume that you are aware drugs are being sold in the school. Does this change your answer to the above question?

3. Will you be able to take any action yet keep Connie's identity secret? How would you accomplish this?

Scenario #14 – Drug Store (Advanced)

1. Were you justified in taking the action you have taken so far, based on the information given to you by Connie Able?
2. Should you at some point have searched the girls and their belongings for contraband? If so, how would you have conducted the search, and whom would you have involved in the search? How intrusive a search would be appropriate under these circumstances?
3. Should you get law enforcement involved? If so, at what point in this situation?
4. Do you think you have the right to search Lisa's car? Are there any prerequisites to doing this? Is searching a student's vehicle under these circumstances legal? If you decide to search Lisa's car, should you do the search, or should law enforcement do the search?
5. Should your immediate supervisor be informed about this situation? Explain.
6. At what point should the parents be notified of what you have done/will do?
7. If a student is found in possession of drugs on school property, what disciplinary action should be taken? Would the type of drug matter? Explain.
8. Stacey has as much as admitted that she sold drugs (or was at least involved in the transaction). What should her school discipline involve?
9. What will your next course of action be in this situation?

Scenario #15 – Out-of-Town Guest

1. Should you give the student's records to this woman?
2. If you ask for identification, what form of identification would be acceptable? Would you need to ask any questions, in addition to seeing some identification, to verify that this woman is the student's parent? Explain.
3. Should you look into the student's permanent file for any information before showing the requested records to this woman? Explain.

Scenario #16 – In the Money Now

1. Is it proper for an account to be set up outside the auspices of the school? Explain.
2. Will Ms. Smith be reprimanded for her actions regarding this account? Explain. If she is reprimanded, what will the reprimand be?
3. Does the fact that this account was set up before you became principal have any bearing on how you handle the situation?
4. Will this situation having come to light change any policies or procedures currently in place in your building? Explain.
5. Assume that this account is improper. Will you need to do anything to ensure that other staff members have not set up and used similar accounts? Explain.

Scenario #17 – Lookin' Mighty Good

1. Now that you know specifically what the boy said and did, would you consider this a sexual harassment case?
2. What disciplinary action, if any, should be taken against the boy?
3. Should the parents of both students be notified of this situation? If so, when?
4. Should this complaint be documented anywhere? If so, where? Would your answer depend on whether this behavior had been considered sexual harassment?

Scenario #18 – Picking on Me (Basic)

1. In retrospect, would you have handled this situation differently from the beginning?
2. This situation obviously requires some immediate action. What should that immediate action be? Should you follow the student out of your office?
3. Once this volatile situation is under control, should Steve receive any discipline for his classroom disruption? Should he receive any discipline for his actions in your office? What do you think the correct discipline, if any, should be? Would your answer be different if this student were being educated under IDEA and his disability had to do with behavior? Explain.

Scenario #19 – Picking on Me (Advanced)

1. In retrospect, would you have handled this situation differently from the beginning? Explain.
2. What should your response to Mr. Stone be? Should he bring Steve back to school today if Steve is found? Explain.
3. In the light of the circumstances Mr. Stone has revealed to you, should Steve receive any discipline for his actions that were directed at you? Should he receive any discipline for his actions in Danielle Potter's class? If Steve should receive discipline, what should it be? Explain the reasoning behind your answers.
4. What will you do if the police contact you and say that they have Steve in custody?
5. Once Steve is back at school, what other available resources might you offer to him and/or his father?
6. Do you think you were threatened by Steve at any time? Explain.

Scenario #20 – Number, Please

1. Should you give Mrs. Kim's telephone number to the officer? Does your positive relationship with Mrs. Kim have any bearing on whether you will provide the telephone number to the police officer? If you decide not to provide the telephone number, what else, if anything, can you do to help the officer?
2. It appears from the information you have that Michelle was truant from school. If she is in major trouble with the police, do you also need to discipline her

at school for her truancy? Does her disposition by the police have any bearing on your answer?

Scenario #21 – Student AIDS

1. Because you have the name of a student who reportedly has AIDS, will you follow up to see whether the report is true?
2. Will you make the schedule change, regardless of whether he actually has AIDS, to calm students' and parents' fears?
3. If any student in your school is identified as having AIDS, what precautions or procedures, if any, should be put into place? Explain.
4. What protections should be afforded a student who is known to have AIDS?
5. How will you respond to this parent at the time of the initial telephone call?

Scenario #22 – a, b, c, D, e, F . .

1. Is it acceptable for the majority of students in a teacher's class to receive Ds or Fs on as many as two major tests? If not, what should be done to correct the problem?
2. If a parent had discovered that many students receive poor grades on Ms. Masterson's tests, what would you have said to that parent?
3. Is Ms. Masterson's answer to why so many students are doing poorly acceptable? Why or why not?
4. Are there any long-term negative consequences to Ms. Masterson's teaching philosophy regarding curriculum topics that must be covered? If so, how can these be addressed?
5. Do you think this teacher needs help? If so, what help can you offer her?

Scenario #23 – Alarmed (Basic)

1. This could be a dangerous situation. What precautions must you take, and when?
2. Should you involve law enforcement? When?
3. At this point, you do not know which student allegedly has a gun. Specifically, how will you go about obtaining this information?
4. Once you have the name of the student who allegedly has a gun in his book bag, how will you approach the student? Will you need anyone else's assistance when you approach the student?
5. On the basis of the information you have and how that information was obtained, should you search the student who allegedly has a gun once you are in a safe place to do so? If so, how intrusive should this search be, and who should conduct the search? What risks would you be taking in conducting a search?
6. At what point in this situation should the student's parents be contacted?
7. If a gun is not found, what should you do? If a gun is found, what should you do?

Scenario #24 – Alarmed (Advanced)

1. Have you taken the correct actions up to this point, or have you overreacted? How could you have handled the situation differently up to this point?
2. Will you talk with Matthew's parents? If so, what will you say to them?
3. What would you have done had the police officers not arrived at that moment? Would the correct action have been for you to enter the classroom and confront the student who you thought had the gun? Explain.
4. Will you question Julian Boles and Mike Mound anymore? Will you need to contact their parents? Explain.
5. Do you need to tell your immediate supervisor and/or the superintendent about this situation? Explain.
6. Has the action taken by you and the police officers been too intrusive in the light of the information you had at the time of the search? Explain.

Scenario #25 – Caught

1. Did you have enough evidence to search Brandon's locker?
2. Can you discipline Brandon for having marijuana at school, considering you had not been looking for it when it was found and he claims it is someone else's? Explain. If Brandon is disciplined, what will his discipline be?
3. Should law enforcement be involved? If so, when?
4. What measures, if any, can be taken to ensure that students do not bring drugs to school?
5. How will you go about finding out who Brandon's friend is (if there really is a "friend")?

Scenario #26 – Emergency

1. Should 911 be called immediately, or should you see whether the student's condition improves first? Should parents be called first if you do decide to call 911?
2. Assume that 911 is called at some point. What information should you be ready with to give the 911 operator?
3. When should parents be called in this situation, and what should you be prepared to tell them? What if you cannot contact the parents?
4. If the student is transported to the hospital and parents have not yet arrived, should someone from school go with the student in the ambulance? Explain.
5. Should you contact your immediate supervisor? Explain.
6. What could be done to ensure that a similar situation does not occur in the future?

Scenario #27 – Loaner

1. You have determined that you will probably have enough copier paper to last the remainder of the school year even if you lend paper to your sister school. Do you need any other information before making your decision?

2. Is it legal and ethical for you to lend paper to another school in your district that was purchased from funds allocated to your building? Do you need permission from the superintendent to lend the paper?

3. Will you lend the paper to Marble Rock Middle School? If you do, would you make any stipulations to Nick Papaganos?

4. If you lend the paper and Nick has not paid it back as he promised by the time school begins the next school year, what should you do?

Scenario #28 – Missing Furniture

1. What other sources might you consider in obtaining furniture in this emergency situation? Can you ask for any help from this vendor? What could you ask this firm to do?

2. What else might you be able to use, in the short run, in lieu of teacher furniture?

3. Will you do business with this vendor in the future? Why or why not?

4. Should your immediate supervisor be informed about this situation? Explain.

Scenario #29 – Nasty Mess (Basic)

1. Should this situation, if the accusations are true, be considered sexual harassment?

2. What would your next course of action be? Should this next action be taken with or without the help of another party?

3. Should law enforcement be contacted in this situation? Explain.

4. Should your immediate supervisor be informed about this situation? Why or why not?

5. If the allegations are true, should David Jones be disciplined? Should he be fired immediately?

Scenario #30 – Nasty Mess (Advanced)

1. Can you grant Jane's request to drop the complaint now? Why or why not?

2. If a situation similar to this involving David had happened several years ago at another school in the district, should David have been fired because of that incident? If he was not fired, should you have known about this incident because David is now working in your building? Would his behavior cause you any concern in regard to students?

3. Even though Jane wants to drop the complaint, do you have enough evidence to discipline David? If David is to be disciplined, what should his discipline be?

4. Does this situation need to be documented? Where should it be documented? Where should the written statements that you already have be filed?

5. Should Bob Browning, the district superintendent, be informed of this most recent turn of events? Should he have input on decisions made in this situation?

6. Has the incident been handled correctly up to this point? Explain.

7. Do you think David's apology to Jane is appropriate at this point, especially considering that you asked him to speak to no one about your conversation with him?

8. Will this situation cause any changes in policies or procedures in your building? Explain.

9. Should law enforcement be contacted in this situation? Explain.

Scenario #31 – Shot in the Arm (Basic)

1. Should Steven have been allowed to attend school up to this point without the shot? Explain.

2. If Mrs. Clark calls to speak with you about this situation, how will you respond to her concern that this is a "silly" reason for Steven not to be allowed to attend school?

3. Can you or the school nurse do anything else to ensure that Steven gets his shot?

4. Are there any legitimate reasons why a student might be allowed to attend school indefinitely without such a shot?

5. Will this situation cause any change in your school's policy regarding shots and how the policy is enforced?

Scenario #32 – Shot in the Arm (Advanced)

1. Should Steven have been allowed to attend school up to this point without the shot?

2. Can you or the school nurse do anything else to ensure that Steven gets his shot?

3. How will you respond to Mrs. Clark's solution to this problem? Should Steven be allowed to attend school on Monday if the exemption papers are delivered as promised? Did Mrs. Clark receive valid information from her friend who told her about religious exemptions? Can you judge whether or not Mrs. Clark truly has religious convictions regarding shots, or do you have to take her word (and documentation) for it? Does the fact that she did not make this declaration more than 2 weeks ago have any bearing on your answer? Explain.

4. Do you need to contact your immediate supervisor regarding this situation? Explain.

5. Will this situation cause any change in your school's policy regarding shots and how the policy is enforced?

Scenario #33 – Trouble Has Arrived, or Has Trouble Arrived?

1. Is there any way you can monitor Bobby's behavior yet allow him to try to improve if he is legitimately trying to do so? Explain.

2. In what other place, if any, could you look to gather information about Bobby? What other information would be beneficial for you to have in dealing with him?

3. Could you get anyone else involved with Bobby and his situation? If so, would you involve individuals, agencies, or both?

4. Knowing what you know about Bobby currently, do you think he poses an immediate danger to students in your school? Do you have enough "hard" evidence to take drastic measures to ensure others' safety?

5. What will you say to Bobby in your meeting with him? Before, during, or after this meeting, will you contact his father?

Scenario #34 – Fire Drill Caper

1. Should you immediately tell the fire chief about the situation at hand? Explain.

2. What other measures can you take to ensure that the missing students have left the building? If you cannot confirm that they have left, what should you do next? Would your procedures be different in the event of an actual fire?

3. Once the students are located, will they be disciplined in any way for not following proper evacuation procedures? Will their parents be contacted? Would it be appropriate to involve the fire chief in speaking with the students?

Scenario #35 – Check It Out

1. Will you be able to give Ms. Gregg an immediate response? If you give a response, what will it be? What will you say if you think you cannot give an immediate response?

2. How important is it to you, the school, and the community that the library meets state standards? Can your school meet accreditation standards with the library in its current condition?

3. Would it be appropriate to cut other building budget areas to meet this need?

4. What other sources of funding, if any, might be used to pay for the library upgrades?

5. If the library can be brought up to standards in a reasonable amount of time, what steps can be taken in the future to ensure that this problem does not happen again?

Scenario #36 – What's Good for the Goose

1. Does the fact that Johnny has an IEP have any bearing on your decision about discipline? Does the number of days that Johnny has already been suspended this year have any bearing on your decision? Does the fact that Sam might miss a basketball tournament have any bearing on your decision? Explain.

2. Will both students receive equal discipline? What discipline will each receive? Explain.

3. Will parents be contacted? When? What will you say to the parents about the discipline their child is receiving? Is it acceptable to say anything about what discipline the other student is receiving? Explain.

4. Should law enforcement be involved? If so, when?

5. Should your immediate supervisor be informed about this situation? Explain.

Scenario #37 – Fizzle

1. Does loyalty to a brand or salesman play into your decision, or should you contract with the company that will give your school the most? Explain.
2. Should your current salesman be informed of what the Rio Cola company is willing to do for your school? Should you ask for sealed proposals from both companies? Explain.
3. Is it moral and ethical for companies to make donations to the school in order to receive contracts to provide services? Explain.
4. The salesman from Rio Cola wants to know what he would have to do to get your business. What will you tell him?

Scenario #38 – For Your Reference

1. Will you need further confirmation, or do you have enough documentation that James was not sick on his third day of absence from work, as he claimed?
2. How will you approach James about this situation? Assuming that you have sufficient documentation of his illegitimate absence, what disciplinary action will you take?
3. Will you need to verify that James was absent for a legitimate reason on the first 2 days of this 3-day absence? If so, how will you verify the legitimacy of these absences?
4. Should your immediate supervisor be made aware of this situation? If your immediate supervisor is not the superintendent, should the superintendent know about this situation?

Scenario #39 – Gone to the Dogs

1. Do you have enough evidence of a drug problem in the school to proceed with some sort of action?
2. In what other way, if any, can you determine which students in your school are "doing" and selling drugs? Explain.
3. If drug dogs are brought to the school, should it be done in the way Detective Ortiz suggests? Explain.
4. Should students and parents be notified before drug dogs are involved in any such endeavor? When and how should parents be notified of any such action?
5. Are any legal issues involved? Could the use of drug dogs in the manner suggested by Detective Ortiz be too intrusive? How else could this issue be addressed?

Scenario #40 – Living in Shangri-La

1. Do you have enough information to assume that Paul does not live in your attendance area? If not, what other information would you need, and how would you go about getting this information?
2. Are any legal issues involved in this situation? Would your answer be any different if Paul were living in your district but attending the wrong school

(assume that Paul is a high school student and that your district has more than one high school)?

3. If you find that Paul is not attending the correct school and does not even live in your district, what should you do?

4. Should the superintendent be informed of this situation? Explain.

Scenario #41 – Unwelcome Visitor

1. Could you have done anything differently up to this point? Explain.

2. What will you do now because the young man is not doing what you ask him to do?

3. Do you need to get law enforcement involved in this situation? If so, at what point?

4. Would it be appropriate to take legal action against this individual, based on what has happened up to this point? Explain.

5. Could any policies or procedures be changed in your school to minimize the possibility of this happening again? Explain.

Scenario #42 – The Accident

1. Is Mr. Stevens's policy regarding passes an acceptable one? Explain.

2. Should you contact Eric's parents? When?

3. Assume that when Eric's parents find out about this they are angry and say that Mr. Stevens's policy is unreasonable. How will you respond?

4. Do any legal issues with regard to this situation concern students' rights?

5. Do you need to do anything to minimize the possibility of a similar situation happening in the future, or do you think this is an isolated incident that does not warrant looking into the school's or the teachers' policies and procedures?

Scenario #43 – Happy Holidays

1. Even though none of the items displayed in the school are truly religious symbols, does their association with Christmas make them religious symbols? Explain.

2. Is this an issue of separation of church and state, as the staff member argues? Explain.

3. What will your answer be to the teacher's request that all holiday decorations be taken down? Explain.

Scenario #44 – What Do I Do Now? (Basic)

1. Even though you have taken several steps in disciplining Andrew, have you missed using any other resources that might be available to you? Explain what those might be.

2. What will be your next disciplinary action taken toward Andrew? Explain.

3. Will Mrs. Weems's note to you have any bearing on what disciplinary action is taken?

Scenario #45 – What Do I Do Now? (Advanced)

1. Will you agree to have a meeting that will include Mrs. Weems?

2. Will you, because of his father's request, agree to reduce the discipline that Andrew has received? If you were to change your decision, how would you explain it to Andrew's teachers? Will Mrs. Weems's attitude have any bearing on whether the disciplinary decision is changed? Would a threat by Mr. Cherio to call the superintendent if the discipline is not significantly reduced have any bearing on your decision?

3. Do you need any more information before making the decisions? If so, what will that information be, and how will you gather it?

4. Should you have done more research before making this disciplinary decision, or was Mrs. Weems's discipline referral and accompanying note enough?

CORWIN
PRESS

The Corwin Press logo—a raven striding across an open book—
represents the happy union of courage and learning. We are a
professional-level publisher of books and journals for K–12 educators,
and we are committed to creating and providing resources that embody
these qualities. Corwin's motto is "Success for All Learners."